Multiparty Politics in America

People, Passions, and Power
Social Movements, Interest Organizations,
and the Political Process
John C. Green, Series Editor

This new series explores the people, activities, and institutions that animate the political process. The series emphasizes recent changes in that process—new actors, new movements, new strategies, new successes (or failures) to enter the political mainstream or influence everyday politics—and places these changes in context with the past and the future. Books in the series combine high quality scholarship with accessibility so that they may be used as core or supplementary texts in upper division political science, sociology, and communication studies courses. The series is consciously interdisciplinary and encourages cross-discipline collaboration and research.

Titles in the Series

Multiparty Politics in America (1997), edited by Paul S. Herrnson and John C. Green

After the Boom: The Politics of Generation X (1997), edited by Stephen C. Craig and Stephen Earl Bennett

The State of the Parties, Second Edition: The Changing Role of Contemporary American Parties (1996), edited by John C. Green and Daniel M. Shea

Forthcoming

Social Movements and American Political Institutions, edited by Ann Costain and Andrew S. McFarland

The Social Movement Society: Comparative Perspectives, edited by David Meyer and Sidney Tarrow

Multiparty Politics in America

Edited by
PAUL S. HERRNSON
and
JOHN C. GREEN

ROWMAN & LITTLEFIELD PUBLISHERS, INC.
Lanham • Boulder • New York • Oxford

ROWMAN & LITTLEFIELD PUBLISHERS, INC.

Published in the United States of America
by Rowman & Littlefield Publishers, Inc.
4720 Boston Way, Lanham, Maryland 20706

12 Hid's Copse Road
Cummor Hill, Oxford OX2 9JJ, England

British Library Cataloguing in Publication Information Available

Library of Congress Cataloging-in-Publication Data

Multiparty politics in America / edited by Paul S. Herrnson and John
C. Green.
    p.   cm.—(People, passions, and power)
    Includes bibliographical references and index.
    ISBN 0-8476-8496-2 (cloth : alk. paper).—ISBN 0-8476-8497-0
(paper : alk. paper)
    1. Political parties—United States.   2. United States—Politics
and government.   I. Herrnson, Paul S., 1958–   .   II. Green, John
Clifford, 1953—   .   III. Series.
JK2261.M85   1997
324.273—dc21   97-18719
                                                                      CIP

ISBN 0-8476-8496-2 (cloth : alk. paper)
ISBN 0-8476-8497-0 (pbk. : alk. paper)

Printed in the United States of America

⊗ ™ The paper used in this publication meets the minimum requirements of
American National Standard for Information Sciences—Permanence of Paper for
Printed Library Materials, ANSI Z39.48–1984.

Contents

Part III: Prospects

Tables and Figures

Tables

Appendix

Figures

Preface

This volume originated in the sixth workshop sponsored by the Political Organizations and Parties Section (POP) of the American Political Science Association in September 1996. The workshop brought together scholars and practitioners to consider the role of minor parties in American party politics. The subject is timely and important for at least two reasons. First, the number of independent and minor party candidates have increased in recent times, a pattern symbolized by Ross Perot and the Reform Party. And second, the possibility of expanded multiparty politics in the United States has captured the imagination of many observers.

This volume and the workshop that inspired it resulted from the hard work of many people. First and foremost, we wish to thank the participants and authors, whose outstanding contributions made both endeavors possible. We also wish to thank the executive committee of POP and the American Political Science Association for sponsoring the workshop. Special thanks go to Kimberly Haverkamp of the Ray C. Bliss Institute of Applied Politics at the University of Akron for preparing the manuscript and to Jennifer Knerr of Rowman & Littlefield for her support, encouragement, and advice.

Other POP workshop publications include: *The Politics of Ideas* (Rowman & Littlefield, 1995), edited by John White; *Representing Interest Groups and Interest Group Representation*, edited by William Crotty and Mildred Schwartz; and *Machine Politics, Sound Bites, & Nostalgia*, edited by Michael Margolis.

Paul Herrnson
John Green

Foreword

Is the Party Over?

David S. Broder

August 9, 1996
The convention that Ross Perot's Reform Party held up the road in Long Beach was treated by the press almost as a footnote to the big news—the selection of Jack Kemp to run with Robert J. Dole on the Republican ticket and the Republican National Convention that may determine whether Dole has a chance to overtake President Clinton in the November election.

But I have a hunch that history will judge the outcome of the Dole–Clinton race to be relatively unimportant and find that the Perot effort, though not of enormous consequence in 1996, will be the launching pad for a third-party candidacy in the year 2000 that could remake our political system.

I say that because the old parties, which will share power in Washington after this election, really have less than two years to deal with a looming national crisis. If they fail, as is likely, one of them, if not both, will be on the way out—and the Reform Party or its equivalent could take over.

Of course, it is customary for politicians to proclaim each presidential election the most important in decades, if not in history. Both Clinton and Dole are applying that superlative to their contest.

It is easy to argue the uniqueness—and therefore the importance—of the November choice. If President Clinton wins, as current polls suggest, he would be the first Democrat elected to a second term since Franklin D. Roosevelt 60 years ago. And it was Roosevelt's second election, even more than his first, that cemented the New Deal coalition that was dominant for so long.

If Dole were to defeat him, as is still possible, he would be the oldest man ever to take the presidential oath and the architect of a

A version of this essay first appeared in the *Washington Post Weekly Edition,* August 19, 1996. Researcher Barbara J. Safir contributed to the original report. © 1996 Washington Post Writers Group. Reprinted with permission.

comeback victory that would match Harry Truman's 1948 upset. It would also signal, as did Ronald Reagan's 1980 victory over President Carter, that this is truly an era of Republican presidents, in which Democrats can hope to win only under fluky circumstances and for only one term at a time.

But odds are that Clinton and Dole are unlikely to define the future of their own parties, much less the nation's. Whichever wins, the prospect is that Republican and Democratic strength in both the House and the Senate will be closely balanced. Absent very strong political, moral and even visionary leadership from the White House, the pattern of intense partisanship we have seen in the last ten years is likely to dominate Capitol Hill.

There may be a brief window of opportunity—most knowledgeable legislators say not more than 18 months—in 1997–98 for Congress and the president to step up to the growing challenge of entitlement reform. Fundamental changes will be needed in Medicare, Medicaid, and Social Security if we are to avert the fiscal calamity that the retirement of the baby boom generation poses for the early years of the next century; and avoid the political upheaval of all-out generational war between those retirees and the working-age men and women whose payroll taxes will skyrocket if no changes are made.

If the politicians elected this November fail to meet the challenge, as the odds suggest, then the stage will be set for the emergence of a serious third-party presidential challenger in the next presidential campaign and the possible replacement of an existing party if its candidate places third.

That prospect seems unlikely to most observers. Historian Alan Brinkley, writing in the July 29 *New Yorker*, noted that it has been a century and a half since the last such substitution occurred—the Republicans replacing the Whigs on the eve of the Civil War.

The most visible third force in today's politics, led by Perot, the eccentric Dallas billionaire, is just a blip on the screen, Brinkley says. "He will not be elected president. . . . The disenchantment and anger he tapped four years ago are not likely to make much difference in November. His Reform Party will probably fade away soon afterward."

But what we have seen in this decade, in the United States and in other democratic countries, should make anyone wary of conventional wisdom. After four decades of remarkable political stability, during which the Democrats dominated Congress and the Republicans held the White House for 28 of 40 years, including 20 of the last 24 and all of the final 12, the 1990s have turned out to be a time of constant political change.

In the first presidential election of the decade, Clinton won a plurality victory over George Bush, and Perot won a bigger share of the vote than any third candidate in 80 years. Two years later, Republicans ended a 40-year run in which Democrats had controlled at least one house of Congress—and usually both. But now, Speaker Newt Gingrich of Georgia, the leader of that Republican Congress, is the least popular well-known politician in the country and his departed congressional partner, Bob Dole, is trailing Clinton by ten points in the latest Washington Post–ABC poll (and by more in some other polls), which also gives Democrats a fair chance of returning to power on Capitol Hill. No governing party seems able to hold public confidence for more than a moment.

What is happening here is not unique to the United States. The last national election in Canada saw the virtual extermination of the long-dominant Conservative Party. In Great Britain, the Tories, who have been in power for 17 years, now trail Labour by 24 points in the polls and face an execution date by May 1997, when the next general election must be held. In this decade, the seven leading industrial democracies, the so-called G-7, have had 23 different heads of government. Japan alone has had six different governments; Italy, seven.

It is not an accident that this decade has seen such political turbulence. Economic, geopolitical and generational changes have combined to apply brutal force to existing parties and voter coalitions.

The introduction to computer technology has remade the workplace for both production and managerial employees, eliminating many jobs and raising the education standards for many more. The virtual erasure of national boundaries to the movement of capital and factories has added to the job anxiety millions feel.

The Cold War has ended, removing what had been the main prop to the entire structure of government and politics since 1946. Public preoccupation with the external threat of expansionist communism has been replaced with a focus on hard-to-solve domestic concerns of unemployment, welfare, crime and drugs.

And the generation that fought in World War II and led through the Cold War has reached the end of the line. Dole would be not only the oldest American president, if elected, but a generation older than most of those governing this and other advanced countries. (Though that younger generation has had the devil's own time sustaining the confidence of its constituents for very long.)

Under these circumstances, and with the psychological impulse of the dawning of a new millennium, it would hardly be surprising to see a new party configuration emerge—and a new party seriously compete for presidency. That will surely be the case if the old parties that will share power after this election fail to address the critical question of entitlement reform. Both the parties have been struggling with serious internal differences: The "new Democrats" of the Democratic Leadership Council vs. the traditionalists in a resurgent labor movement and the vital minority and senior-citizen constituency groups; the Christian Coalition and its allies vs. the libertarian, suburban and Main Street Republicans.

But it takes a major issue to force a political realignment, and the entitlement crunch is one that affects enough people—literally, the entire society—to fill that role. The Medicare trust fund, as everyone knows, will be exhausted by 2001, the year the president we elect in November will finish his term. The Social Security system is in no position to cope with the wave of baby boomer retirements starting in the years from 2005 to 2010. As the Kerrey–Danforth bipartisan commission has reported, by the year 2010, Medicare, Medicaid, and Social Security, plus interest on the debt, will consume almost every dollar of taxes the current revenue system will produce, leaving a choice between deep cuts in defense and domestic spending or ruinously high taxes on working families.

What has been a matter of speculation could easily become a reality—an explosive battle between the generations, as the boomer retirees insist on the benefits they have been promised and the post-boomer workers refuse to ante up.

In their non-campaign moments (which are few and far between) Clinton and Dole both realize this. Either one, in the White House, might act on the knowledge that the only way to avert the crisis is to rise above partisanship and try to build a middle-road coalition of support for the needed changes from members of both parties on Capitol Hill.

That is a possibility, and if the House and Senate remain closely divided between the parties, cooperation between the parties and with the president may recommend itself as the best strategy for Gingrich and Senate Majority Leader Trent Lott of Mississippi and for their Democratic counterparts, Representative Dick Gephardt of Missouri and Senator Tom Daschle of South Dakota.

The recent successes of compromise health and welfare legislation have encouraged these hopes. But those issues were easy, compared with the political challenge of the larger entitlement reform that lies ahead. The health care bill was a minimalist effort that left the fundamental problems of the system—the growing millions of uninsured and the rising costs of medical services—unsolved. And the famous welfare compromise essentially hands the problem over to the states, with less money to solve it. Those easy-outs are not available when it comes to the big federal entitlement programs.

Dole conspicuously dodged the issue in presenting his economic blueprint two weeks ago. In fact, he promised to "protect" Medicare and Social Security from the spending cuts that will be necessary to pay for his proposed tax breaks. And Clinton has profited mightily by demagoguing the earlier GOP efforts to slow the spending increases in Medicare and Medicaid.

It is by no means clear that either Dole or Clinton would have much leverage to force congressional action on the entitlements, were he so inclined. Dole is tolerated, rather than deferred to, by Gingrich and Lott and their fellow revolutionaries in the GOP, who realize that their presidential candidate is temperamentally and generationally at a distance from the movements that have reshaped their party in the last two decades. And Clinton has yet to prove he can hold to a steady course of leadership for more than a short period. His tendency to zigzag ideologically and try to please the crowd is very strong. Half the Democrats in Congress, including the party leaders in the House and Senate, broke with him on the compromise welfare bill, openly accusing him of playing election-year politics for his own benefit.

Democrats on Capitol Hill worry publicly that the problems he has managed to postpone past this November's election—the Paula Jones case, the investigations by Whitewater special prosecutor Kenneth Starr and more possible indictments—may all come raining down early in a second term.

If Clinton is reelected, history argues strongly for Republican congressional gains in 1998 (the party opposing the president has averaged 43 House seats and eight Senate seats gained in the midterm elections that occur six years after a president has taken office). Gingrich and Lott may well decide just to out wait Clinton. And there is no assurance of harmony between congressional Democrats and their lame-duck president. Indeed, all the talk among party insiders assumes that Gephardt and Vice President Al Gore will start battling for the succession the day after the 1996 election is settled.

Voters may wish for an end to gridlock and partisanship on Capitol Hill, but historical forces make that unlikely as long as the choice of candidates is limited to the existing parties. Each of those parties has grown more internally homogeneous. With the voting rights revolution, the old-style conservative Southern Democrats have almost disappeared from the scene. Those seats are now occupied either by liberal black Democrats or, more often, by conservative white Republicans.

At the same time, the tradition of moderate or liberal Republicans from the Northeast and Midwest also has become frayed. When I wrote recently about the virtual disappearance of this valuable breed, John Chafee, the Republican senator from Rhode Island who has worked so hard to keep his party a positive force on environmental and social issues, gently reminded me that he and a few others were still around. They are, but they are only a corporal's guard in a party much more ideologically conservative than it has ever been.

Reinforcing the polarization between the parties are the pressures that their predominant interest groups exert. Those interest groups have become even more important on Capitol Hill, as party discipline has weakened. And the dominant interest groups of the Republican and Democratic parties are enemies in a way that the parties themselves never were.

Unions really have flexed their financial muscle for the congressional Democrats: a $35 million dues-financed advertising campaign, plus untold millions more in voluntary contributions, plus hundreds of field organizers working on Democratic campaigns. But their role is almost matched by that of the small-business groups in the Republican Party. In the last few years, the National Federation of Independent Business has become perhaps the most important source of grassroots support for Republican candidates. R. Marc Nuttle, a onetime director of Republican congressional campaigns, has trained and recruited hundreds of candidates, campaign managers, fundraisers and canvassers through the NFIB. The NFIB agenda is diametrically opposed to that of organized labor, not just on pocketbook issues like the minimum wage but on a whole range of social programs as well.

A similar confrontation looms between the religious conservative organizations, like the Christian Coalition, now deeply involved in setting strategy and focusing the agenda for Republicans, and the liberal feminist groups, which exercise comparable influence among the Democrats. On abortion and a host of other issues, there is little room for compromise among these groups—and therefore heavy odds against bipartisanship becoming the prevailing pattern in the next Congress. These interest groups have a huge investment in the Republicans and Democrats and will do all in their power to prevent a new party from emerging. But the alliance between the interest groups and those parties is an equally huge negative in the eyes of many voters.

The years 1997–98 loom as Last Chance Gulch for the old parties. By the end of 1996, all the conditions will be in place for a new party to emerge. Ross Perot's money and ambition will give ballot status to the Reform Party in virtually all the states. Without doing more than an occasional television appearance these past six months, Perot has held about 15 percent of the vote in trial heats against Clinton and Dole. The likelihood is that whatever happens to Perot in November (or to former Colorado Governor Richard Lamm, should he unexpectedly win the Reform Party nomination), that party will this year establish itself as a permanent feature on the political landscape, with $25 million or $30 million in public funding and ballot position awaiting whomever its nominee may be in the year 2000.

And there is no shortage of people who might lead such a party. Indeed, you could form a presidential ticket and organize a government at least as talented as any we have seen in the last half-century in Washington simply from Democrats and Republicans who have dropped out of leadership positions in the last few years—mainly because of their own frustration with partisan gridlock in Washington or the forces that have come to dominate their own party.

Bill Bradley, John Danforth, Warren Rudman, George Mitchell, William Cohen, Paul Simon, Nancy Kassebaum, Gary Hart, Paul Tsongas are just a few of those who have left early—but might be lured back. You could add at least as many notable names of former House members and former governors and mayors.

Democratic Senator Sam Nunn of Georgia, one of the most notable of this year's dropouts, spoke for many of them in an exchange on *Meet the Press* July 21. When NBC's Tim Russert asked Nunn about "the third-party threat" in this election, Nunn said: "I think both major parties, Democrats and Republicans in the two-party system, have served our nation well for years. But I believe we're in a new period, and I think both parties have defaulted in . . . long-term fiscal leadership. I don't think either party is looking down the road 15 or 20 years. . . .

"So we're going to have a third party this year, under Perot or whomever the Reform Party chooses. I don't think they'll win. But if they bring a message about what we have to do for our children and grandchildren, they'll be serving a real role. And unless we have some campaign reform and some long-term fiscal reform, I see we're going to have a third party in the future without any doubt."

Russert asked, "Would you ever think in the future of heading up a third party or being involved with a third party?"

Nunn, who has challenged the prevailing liberalism in his own party often enough that some Republicans even suggested him as a Dole running-mate, said, "Well, I've always been sort of a bad Democrat, and if I joined the Republican Party, I'd be a bad Republican. So maybe there is a third party out there in my future."

I believe there is such a party in the nation's near future. I came into political journalism 40 years ago with a strong belief that the two-party system is a vital and irreplaceable bulwark of our system of government. I still believe that. But public dissatisfaction with the performance of the Democrats and Republicans is simply too great to be ignored. The old parties have one last chance to get it done—and get it right. Otherwise the retirement-wave, health care and pension crisis that is coming on us will create a shock large enough to alter our party system.

The Civil War and the Great Depression did that. The prospect of generational warfare and financial ruin could do the same thing. If nothing happens to relieve the pressure in the next two years, the new millennium is likely to produce a new political era.

Introduction

Making or Repeating History?
American Party Politics at the
Dawn of a New Century

Paul S. Herrnson and John C. Green

Is the United States in the process of developing a viable, multiparty system? This question is being asked with increasing frequency by a wide range of observers. That such a question is raised at all is interesting, given the long dominance of the two-party system. Leaving aside the novelty of the idea, the notion of a multiparty system has become plausible for two reasons. First, the two-party system seems incapable of resolving the policy crises of the 1990s, and second, disaffected activists are turning to minor parties at an unusually high rate.

Worries over the capacity of the two-party system to cope with the pressing national problems are now commonplace. David Broder's essay that serves as the foreword to this book is a good example. Echoing the title of his well-known book *The Party's Over* (1970), Broder argues that the major parties have "one last chance to get it done—and get it right" on a host of critical issues, especially health care, pensions, and other entitlements. Failure to resolve these problems, argues Broder, will open the door for a new era, led by a new political party, and perhaps a new kind of party system.

Particularly troubling is the recent wave of retirements by moderates in both major parties, many in mid-career. The likes of Democrats Sam Nunn and Bill Bradley and Republicans Bill Cohen and Nancy Kassebaum Baker are the types of leaders who historically have given the major parties their capacity to make the compromises needed to enact legislation. These politicians are now on the sidelines—and potentially available to lead a new party. When coupled with declining voter loyalty, disgust with the political process, and disappointment with the 1996 campaign, the breakdown of major party politics appears to be increasingly plausible.

The 1990s were a period of intense minor party activity. In 1996, a total of seventeen minor party candidates, representing some thirty parties, ran for president. The candidates for the Reform and Libertarian parties appeared on the ballot in all fifty states and the District of Columbia, while candidates for the Natural Law, U.S. Taxpayers, and Green parties appeared on the ballots in forty-four, thirty-nine, and twenty-two states, respectively.[1] The remaining twelve candidates appeared on twelve state ballots or fewer, with eight appearing on fewer than five. All together, minor parties gained a respectable 10 percent of the vote.

The 1996 election came on the heels of other challenges from minor parties. In 1992, Perot won 19 percent of the vote, an eighty-year high for an independent or minor party candidate. There were similar occurrences for lower-level offices: Lowell Weicker's election as an independent governor of Connecticut, Walter Hickel's similar feat for governor of Alaska, and independent Representative Bernard Sanders's ability to win and retain a seat in the U.S. House of Representatives from Vermont. Minor party activity expanded dramatically in state legislative and local races as well.

While few observers doubt the severity of the problems facing the country, many are skeptical that profound changes in the party system will occur anytime soon. After all, the Democrats and Republicans garnered most of the 1992 and 1996 vote and still dominate every state and local government in the country. The two-party system has faced even greater strains in the past and has shown an extraordinary capacity to adapt. Disaffection and disgust are the normal results of difficult political choices, and minor parties are just one of many expressions of these concerns. Indeed, if the past is any guide, the major parties will eventually be reconfigured and revitalized, preserving the two-party character of the system intact.

Will the present situation lead to genuine multiparty politics? Or will the two-party system adjust to these pressures? Put another way, will history be made or will history repeat itself? This book examines these questions from a number of different perspectives. Written by noted scholars, political observers, and practitioners, the chapters presented here consider the possibilities, performance, and prospects for multiparty politics in America as a new century begins.

These essays beg an important question, however: what constitutes a minor party? A useful perspective is offered by Leon Epstein, who defines a political party as "any group, however loosely organized, seeking to elect government office-holders under a given label" and then goes on to point out that "conceivably, even one man seeking office could similarly adopt a label and qualify as a party"(1980: 9).

From this perspective, a minor party is any group that seeks to elect officials under a common label, but that has not been successful enough to govern directly at present, in the past, or in the near future. This approach allows for genuinely independent candidacies (those who do not run under any label), but does not disqualify electoral efforts from consideration as parties on the basis of success, goals, structure, strategy, or activity level. As Epstein argues: "No matter how small the vote or how special the occasion, no minor party is so minor as not generically to be a party" (1980: 11). While not all scholars would accept this definition of a minor party (cf. Sartori 1976; Smith 1991; Mair 1991), it provides the widest scope for investigating party politics. And as we will see below, the variety of minor parties is extraordinary, even within the context of the American "two-party" system.[2]

Possibilities

The chapters in Part I review the possibilities for minor parties, starting with Paul Herrnson's historical and analytic review of American party politics (chapter 1). He addresses two fundamental questions: what are the sources of the American two-party system, and what role do minor parties play in party politics? Herrnson finds that "major party dominance" is deeply rooted in American electoral institutions and behavioral tendencies, so much so that its basic structure has endured numerous periods of intense stress. Periodic "minor party forays" are best thought of as an integral part of the two-party structure, relieving such stresses and bolstering the two-party system rather than undermining or replacing it. Herrnson describes four types of minor parties: enduring comprehensive, candidate-focused, single-issue, and fusion parties. While their impacts vary, there is little prospect that such parties will produce genuine multiparty politics.

The subsidiary role of American minor parties has long interested scholars because it is unlike what occurs in most other democracies. Why and how do American minor parties differ from their counterparts elsewhere? Robert Harmel addresses these questions in his review of new minor parties in Europe, and he makes several important observations. First, minor parties are just as numerous in the United States as in European countries. Second, new minor parties have a high rate of failure everywhere. Third, American minor parties do the worst, rarely winning anything, a situation largely attributable to the American electoral institutions. Finally, American minor parties are issue "promoters" rather than electoral "contenders," advancing issues to "influence" rather than to capture the government. Like Herrnson, Harmel suggests that genuine multiparty politics is unlikely in America, and minor party agitation will probably continue.

These surveys of the American and European scenes suggest that history will repeat itself: that minor parties will contribute to the resolution of the crises of the 1990s within the context of the two-party system. Other observers are less sure, and in any event, believe the time is ripe to make history by pursuing fundamental institutional changes that will create a multiparty system. To this end, a small but vocal group of activists, scholars, and reform organizations are pressuring the federal, state, and even some local governments to revise their election codes in ways that would benefit minor parties at the expense of their major party counterparts. These reformers argue that without current restrictions on minor parties, from ballot access limitations to plurality elections, a multiparty system would emerge and flourish in the United States.

In chapter 3, Kay Lawson makes a strong case for a multiparty system that is consistent with this position. First, she argues that a multiparty system is more "natural." That is, in the absence of restriction, many political parties will organize and contest elections, a point supported by Harmel's findings on new party creation. Second, she claims that most legal limits on minor parties constitute an unacceptable infringement on political rights of the citizenry. Third, she suggests that a multiparty system is more democratic, in the sense of both protecting minorities and representing majorities. Commonly cited defects in multiparty politics, she points out, can be remedied by modest regulations.

Lawson then presents a number of reforms that would extend "multipartyism" in the United States. Some would abolish existing regulations, such as ballot access laws, and others would impose new regulations, such as prohibiting private financing of campaigns. But the most important involves fundamental institutional changes: the implementation of proportional representation. In this sense, Lawson's argument supports Herrnson's findings that the two-party system is largely rooted to the structure of American elections.

Lawson's case for a multiparty system rests on a particular conception of democracy, one that is popular throughout the world, but not common in the United States. Minor party activists and scholars who prefer a multiparty system have brought this new view of democracy into American politics. In contrast, political activists and scholars who support the American two-party system couch their arguments in terms of a different conception of democracy, one popular in the United States. They are also more concerned with the operation of the political system in the unique American context. While not necessarily supportive of all current restrictions on minor parties, this larger group of observers are not troubled by the basic two-party biases of American electoral institutions. The major parties, after all, are representative of most citizens, and have served well the causes of majority rule and self-government. Reforms that give special treatment to minor parties are considered unfair and undemocratic.

In chapter 4, John Bibby offers a forthright defense of the two-party system. He admits that the American system does routinely limit the choices before the electorate, but that, on the whole, this limitation is beneficial. First, the two-party process builds legitimacy for elected officials. Second, two-party politics is an effective mechanism for achieving national unity, reconciliation, and policy moderation. And third, the two-party system fosters electoral accountability and more effective governance. Commonly cited defects in American parties, Bibby concludes, are often overstated, and reformers should focus on strengthening the system rather than replacing it.

Bibby also considers the two-party system to be rooted in American electoral institutions. But instead of viewing such arrangements as restrictions on political freedom, Bibby points out that major party politics in the United States are among the freest and most open in the world. The direct primary and other features of the system give party members and voters a great deal of influence—at the expense of party leaders. While citizens frequently voice dissatisfaction with the performance of the major parties, they are appreciative of a system that gives them numerous avenues to register their discontentment. Minor parties are just one such means, Bibby notes, and their impact is frequently exaggerated. Here, Bibby argues with Herrnson and Harmel that minor parties are adjuncts to the two-party system.

Performance

Lawson and Bibby address fundamental questions: what are the relative advantages and disadvantages of two-party and multiparty systems? Central to the answers they give are assumptions about the nature of minor parties, with Lawson appreciating their performance under difficult circumstances and Bibby expressing skepticism about the impact of their efforts. But how have minor parties performed in the United States? The chapters in Part II look at the performance of American minor parties in recent times.

In chapter 5, John Green and William Binning take a hard look at the founding and future of the Reform party, which along with its leader, Ross Perot, has encouraged much of the recent speculation about multiparty politics. In Herrnson's terms, the Reform party is a candidate-focused party, and in Harmel's terms, an issue promoter. The Reform party seems to have performed many of the functions Lawson expects of minor parties, but did so by means she is skeptical of, such as private wealth and media attention. And Perot appears to have had more of an impact than Bibby assigns to minor parties, but mostly on the major parties themselves.

Green and Binning argue that the future of the Reform party depends on "surviving Perot." On this score, much of the evidence, which is rooted in the origins of the party, is not encouraging. The Reform party was and still is largely a creature of Perot, drawing on his personal appeal and assets. While Perot was a potent vehicle for protest, he was not viewed as a plausible alternative by most Americans. A study of Reform party activists in Ohio confirms this point: these activists are largely a personal following of their founder. However, the special circumstances of 1992 and 1996 gave the Reform party a host of resources not generally available to minor parties, from ballot access to committed activists to federal financing. Thus, these authors conclude, it is possible, though perhaps not probable, for the Reform party to become a viable minor party.

This conclusion is expanded upon in chapter 6, Christian Collet's discussion on minor party candidates in subnational politics. He begins by documenting the dramatic rise in minor party activity in recent times, noting that this "abnormal route" to politics is becoming increasingly common. Collet next provides a useful typology of minor parties in terms of their substantive content. He first distinguishes between "old left" and "old right," which partake of the old economic cleavage in national politics, and "new left" and "new right" parties, which represent new "postmaterial" divisions. Then he identifies a "centrist" category that represents moderate refugees from present-day alignments. In Herrnson's terms, the former categories are a mix of enduring comprehensive and single-issues parties, while the latter are largely candidate-focused. In Harmel's terms, most of these parties are issue promoters.

Collet's evidence on the backgrounds, beliefs, and activities addresses the question: What are minor party supporters like? The short answer is they are quite diverse, providing food for critics and defenders of the two-party system, but this diversity is encapsulated within the patterns observed by Herrnson and Harmel. He finds that while minor party candidates resemble their major party counterparts in demographic terms, they are quite different politically. Few strongly identify with their parties. Most value political independence and easily locate themselves within the two-party framework. Most are inexperienced politically and are not particularly active even in their own campaigns. Finally, many are fierce ideologues, holding policy positions sharply at variance with most of the public. This raises an important question: are the weaknesses of these candidates due to the unfavorable political environment, or are they fundamental to minor party politics?

One place to look for answers to this and other questions is in the closest thing to a multiparty system operating in the United States today: the New York system of partisan "cross-endorsements." Robert Spitzer (chapter 7) provides a cogent description of this unusual system, which is built on "fusion," a system whereby candidates can be nominated by more than one party and have their names on several different ballot lines. Although minor parties must earn ballot position by petition or votes for their gubernatorial candidate, they can then bestow their nominations on their own or even major party candidates. Spitzer argues that this "near-multiparty system" offers an avenue for invigorated party politics. Indeed, many advocates of multiparty politics look to fusion as a potent tool and advocate its expansion nationwide.

Prospects

Part III looks at the prospects for minor parties in the near future. This section begins with chapters by three minor party leaders, representing the Libertarian, Reform, and Green parties. The Green and Libertarian parties are good examples of Collet's "new left" and "new right" parties, respectively, while the Reform party is centrist. The first two are good examples of enduring comprehensive parties, in Herrnson's terms, while the latter is, of course, candidate-focused. All three are issue promoters in Harmel's analytic framework. It is interesting to note, however, that neither Terry Savage of the Libertarian party (chapter 8) nor Greg Jan of the Green party (chapter 10) thinks of his organization exclusively as an issue promoter. While their distinctive ideologies are critical to their party activity, each is strongly pragmatic, seeking to make his party an electoral contender and winner at the polls. Similarly, Justin Roberts of the Reform party (chapter 9) does not think of his party as candidate-focused, but rather as an issue-driven movement in response to major party failure.

All of these leaders stress the enormous legal obstacles minor parties regularly face. Richard Winger, the editor of *Ballot Access News*, describes these obstacles in greater detail (chapter 11). Using minor party victories since 1945 as a measure of minor party success, Winger identifies five features of state law that help account for such success: (1) freedom to nominate recent converts, (2) opportunities for fusion, (3) lenient ballot access requirements, (4) reasonable nomination procedures, and (5) low filing fees. Most state election laws lack these features, confirming some of Lawson's concerns about restrictions on minor party activity.

Winger's theme is expanded upon in chapter 12 by Diana Dwyre and Robin Kolodny, which draws upon the previous chapters to provide a comprehensive review of the barriers to minor parties and prospects for change. These authors identify three kinds of barriers: cultural biases, legal obstacles, and institutional hurdles. Some of these barriers represent fundamental institutional structures and attitudes that support the two-party system of the sort identified by Herrnson and Harmel. Other barriers are less fundamental in nature, including laws and practices that interfere with the ability of minor parties to participate in elections, just the sorts of problems that trouble Lawson and Winger. But, whatever their sources and impact, Dwyre and Kolodny see little prospect for major change in the short run. They suggest that, at most, a few modest alterations could be enacted that would promote long-term effects.

This conclusion was borne out by a Supreme Court decision handed down as this manuscript was going to press (April 28, 1997). In *Timmons et al. v. Twin Cities Area New Party,* a case mentioned in virtually every chapter in this book because of its potential impact on minor parties, the Court addressed the constitutionality of state anti-fusion laws currently in force in forty states (see chapters 7 and 11 for a fuller discussion of fusion tickets and anti-fusion laws). By a six to three margin, the Supreme Court upheld the Minnesota law prohibiting fusion tickets. Writing for the majority, Chief Justice William Rehnquist argued that state governments have a constitutional right to regulate elections and that anti-fusion laws do not violate the First Amendment rights of minor parties as alleged in the suit. (By the same logic, existing state laws permitting fusion tickets are also constitutional.)

Acknowledging the bias of anti-fusion laws in favor of the two-party system, Rehnquist argued: "The Constitution permits the Minnesota Legislature to decide that political stability is best served through a healthy two-party system." In dissent, Justice John Paul Stevens took issue with this position: "It demeans the strength of the two-party system to assume that the major parties need to rely on laws that discriminate against independent voters and minor parties to preserve their strength." Defenders of the two-party system are no doubt pleased by

Rehnquist's argument, while advocates of multipartyism surely favor Steven's position.[3]

We leave to the readers the questions we posed at the outset. Will the problems identified by David Broder and others lead to genuine multiparty politics in America? Or will the two-party system adjust to these pressures, as it has in the past, perhaps with the aid of minor parties? Will history be made or will history repeat itself?

Notes

1. John Hagelin, the Natural Law party nominee, also appeared on the ballot as an independent in four states; Howard Phillips, the U.S. Taxpayer party nominee, also appeared on the ballot as the nominee of the Taxpayers party, several statewide taxpayer parties, the American Independent party, the Concerned Citizens party, the Right-to-Life party, or as an independent in twenty-four states; and Ralph Nader, the Green party nominee, appeared on the ballot as the nominee of several statewide Green parties, the Pacific party, the Liberty, Ecology, and Community party, or as an independent in eight states.

2. We wish to thank Christian Collet for these citations.

3. We are indebted to Richard Winger, editor of *Ballot Access News,* for information on this case.

Part I

Possibilities

1

Two-Party Dominance and Minor Party Forays in American Politics

Paul S. Herrnson

The United States has experienced numerous minor party and independent candidacies over the course of its history. Minor party (or third-party) candidates have run for offices ranging from city council to president. A small number, including the former governor of Connecticut, Lowell Weicker, and the U.S. representative from Vermont, Bernard Sanders, have been successful. Others, like Theodore Roosevelt, who was the Progressive (or Bull Moose) party's presidential nominee in 1912, won significant numbers of votes and influenced the outcome of an election, but failed to get elected. More common, however, was the experience of Margaret Byrnes, who in 1994 ran for New York's eighth congressional district seat under the Conservative party label and received only 2 percent of the vote.

The success rates and political influence of minor parties are no better or worse than those of their candidates. The parties' limited success, and the ability of the two major parties to monopolize power, places the United States in a relatively small group of modern democracies that are classified as having two-party rather than multiparty systems. The first section of this chapter describes the historical continuity of two-party dominance and analyzes the institutional structures and behavioral norms that provide its foundations. The second section analyzes the types of minor parties that have participated in American politics, the conditions that help them garner support, and their roles in American politics. The chapter concludes with comments on the limitations and contributions of minor parties in the two-party system.

The Two-Party System

American politics have almost always been dominated by two parties. Major parties differ from their minor party counterparts in a variety of ways, including the sizes and compositions of their followings, their pragmatism in selecting issues and candidates, their location on the ideological spectrum, the types and amounts of politically relevant resources under their control, and the number of offices their candidates contest. Perhaps the most important difference between major and minor parties concerns power. As a result of recent successes at the polls, the major parties have sufficient numbers of public officeholders to exercise substantial power over the nation's political agenda and the policy-making processes. Although a few minor parties elect some of their members to public office, they do not qualify as major parties because they do not control enough elective offices, or have not done so in the recent past, to be contenders for power.

Historical Development

The seeds for the two-party system were sown during the Colonial era and firmly rooted by the time the Federalists and Anti-Federalists battled over ratification of the U.S. Constitution. Since then, the nation's political history has been largely defined by five separate party eras or party systems (e.g., Burnham 1970; Bibby 1987, 21–34).

Under the first party era, the Federalists and the Democratic Republicans battled over whether the nation should develop into a commercial republic or remain a largely agrarian society. The Federalists, who were primarily supported by landowners, merchants, and other established families of the Northeast and Atlantic regions, favored a strong national government. The Democratic Republican party, which was founded by Thomas Jefferson, attracted small farmers, workers, and others of modest means. It championed the extension of suffrage, decentralized power, and other ideals of popular self-government. Although the Federalists won the nation's first contested presidential election, the party's narrow base prevented it from again capturing the White House and resulted in its disintegration.

The second period of two-party competition began following a short period of one-party dominance that was characterized by bifactional politics within the Democratic Republican party. This era, which lasted from 1836 into the 1850s, pitted the Democratic party of Andrew Jackson against the Whigs, who were led by Henry Clay and Daniel Webster. Both parties were broad-based popular parties. The Democrats were primarily aligned with the interests of frontiersmen, immigrants, and other less privileged voters. The Whigs attracted more support from manufacturers, trading interests, and citizens of Protestant stock. Conflicts over slavery led to the second party system's demise.

The slavery issue cut across existing party cleavages and led to the formation of several short-lived minor parties, the birth of the modern Republican party, and ultimately the start of the third party era. Lincoln's successful prosecution of the Civil War led the Republican party to be identified with victory, patriotism, reconstruction, and the abolition of slavery. The party was also identified with a concern for mercantile and propertied interests. The Republicans drew their support from the North and West, while their Democratic opponents enjoyed strong support in the South. The Democratic party also attracted significant votes from Roman Catholics who lived in northern cities.

The 1896 election marked the dawning of the fourth party era and a new period of Republican dominance in national politics. William McKinley, the Republican standard-bearer, increased support for his party in northeastern cities and among the population in general. Democratic (and Populist) nominee William Jennings Bryan's campaign to expand the money supply attracted support from farmers in the South and the Plains states and silver miners in the West. It failed, however, to win many votes from the industrial centers of the East and Midwest. McKinley defeated Bryan twice and the GOP won every presidential contest from 1896 through 1932, except for Wilson's two victories, the first of which was largely the result of Theodore Roosevelt's minor party candidacy.

The Great Depression and the election in 1932 launched the fifth party era. President Herbert Hoover and his fellow Republicans received the brunt of the blame for the nation's economic woes. In 1932 and over the course of the next decade, Franklin Roosevelt and the Democrats pieced together a majority coalition comprised of blue-collar workers, urban dwellers, Southerners, ethnic minorities, and blacks. The Democratic and Republican parties battled over the federal government's role in the economy and the welfare state. During the 1960s, civil rights and a variety of social issues began to erode the original economic foundation of the New Deal coalition and contributed to the election of several Republican presidents. Whether the election of a Republican-controlled Congress in 1994 marks the beginning of a sixth party system remains a matter of debate (Beck 1997, 13–136; Aldrich and Niemi 1996).

Institutional Foundations

Institutional arrangements have played a major role in perpetuating the U.S. two-party system. The Constitution is challenging to political parties in general, but particularly inhospitable to minor parties. Federalism, the separation of powers, and bicameralism provide a strong foundation for candidate-centered politics and impede party-focused election efforts, especially the efforts of parties that do not enjoy a broad constituent base.

Single-member, simple-plurality elections, which are not delineated in the Constitution, also make it very difficult for minor parties to have a major impact on elections or policy making (Duverger 1954, 217). This winner-take-all system denies any elected offices to candidates or parties that do not place first in an election, even when the party garners a significant share of the national vote or runs a close second in several contests. This is especially harmful to minor parties, which are usually considered successful when their candidates place second at the polls. By depriving minor parties of seats in Congress or state legislatures, ensuring that few of their members become presidents or governors, and depriving their supporters of judgeships, cabinet posts, and other forms of patronage, the electoral system discourages their institutional development and growth. Most minor parties survived for only a relatively short time because of their inability to play a significant role in governing.

The Electoral College poses particular difficulties for minor parties. The contest for the nation's highest office actually consists of fifty-one separate elections—one held in each of the states and the District of Columbia. In order to win any Electoral College votes, a presidential candidate needs to capture a majority of votes in at least one state or the District. Winning the election requires a candidate to win a majority of Electoral College votes.[1] Nationally based minor parties, such as the Libertarian party, may win a significant share of the popular vote, but they rarely receive enough support to capture a state's electoral votes. Regional minor parties, such as the Dixiecrat (or States' Rights) party, which nominated then Democratic Senator Strom Thurmond of South Carolina in 1948, may win the popular vote in a number of states. However, because their vote is concentrated in those states, these parties often win more popular votes than they need to win Electoral College votes from states in their region and too few popular votes to capture Electoral College votes elsewhere. Their failure to capture political offices does little to help minor parties expand their bases of support or survive for long periods.

Institutional recognition also gives the two major parties ballot access advantages over minor parties. Because they receive automatic placement on the ballot, the two major parties are able to focus most of their energies on winning the support of voters. In many states, minor party and independent candidates can only remain on the ballot by winning a threshold of votes. Those that receive fewer are treated like new parties: to qualify for a place on the ballot they may need to pay a filing fee or submit a minimum number of signatures to local or state election officials prior to the general election or, in some cases, the primary contest (Winger 1995).

The number of signatures required to gain access to the ballot varies widely across the states. In New Jersey, a minor party candidate needs to collect a mere 800 signatures to qualify as a candidate for the Senate, whereas in Florida one needs 196,788. Moreover, minor parties that wish to compete in all fifty states are often penalized at lower ends of the ballot. In 1996, a minor party needed to collect roughly 750,000 signatures to secure a place on the ballot for its presidential candidate in all fifty states, but had to gather more than 1.6 million signatures to place its House candidates on the ballot in all 435 congressional districts (Jost 1995, 1143).

Participatory nominations enable the major parties to absorb protest and discourage the formation of minor parties (Epstein 1986, 129–132). State-regulated caucuses and state-administered primaries give dissident groups from outside or inside the party the opportunity to run candidates for a major party nomination, thereby discouraging them from forming new minor parties.

The campaign finance system also penalizes minor parties. The Federal Election Campaign Act of 1974 and its amendments (collectively referred to as the FECA) provide subsidies for major party candidates for the presidency. During the 1996 presidential election, candidates for major party nominations who raised $5,000 in individual contributions of $250 or less in at least twenty states qualified for up to $15.45 million in federal matching funds, enabling them to spend $37.92 million to contest the nomination. Minor party candidates can also qualify for matching funds, if they meet the same requirements as their major party counterparts. As a practical matter, however, these requirements are easily met by serious major party nomination candidates, but pose substantial barriers to minor party contestants because of the lack of support their parties enjoy among individuals who make campaign contributions.

Major parties also automatically receive funds to help them pay for their national conventions. In 1996, the Democratic and Republican national committees each received just over $12.36 million for that purpose. Minor parties can also qualify for convention subsidies, but only if their presidential nominee garners 5 percent or more of the popular vote in the previous presidential election.[2] A minor party has yet to qualify for convention funding under the FECA.

The FECA also provides substantial federal grants to major party presidential nominees. In 1996, President Bill Clinton and former

Senator Bob Dole each received $61.8 million to wage their general election campaigns. Minor party and independent candidates can also qualify for federal funding in the general election, but they typically receive much smaller amounts. Newly emergent minor parties and first-time presidential candidates can only qualify for federal subsidies retroactively. Candidates who receive more than 5 percent of the popular vote are rewarded with campaign subsidies, but only after the election when it is too late to have any impact on the outcome. Minor parties that have made a good showing in a previous election automatically qualify for campaign subsidies during the current contest, but they get only a fraction of the money given to the major parties. Ross Perot's 19 percent of the popular vote in 1992 qualified him for $29.2 million in federal funds in 1996. His acceptance of those funds severely limited his ability to compete because he began with fewer funds than his major party opponents, could contribute a maximum of $50,000 to his own campaign, and had to stay within the legal contribution limits when trying to make up his campaign's $32.6 million deficit.

Minor party candidates who cannot or choose not to finance their own campaigns are severely handicapped because of the legal limits on contributions they can collect from others. Ceilings of $1,000 for individuals and $5,000 for political action committees (PACs) prohibit minor party candidates from underwriting their campaigns with large contributions from a small group of backers. Ceilings on party contributions and expenditures also limit the extent to which candidates can depend on a minor party for support. The modest levels of public support that most minor party candidates enjoy make it virtually impossible for them to raise large sums in the form of small donations. Only a few extremely wealthy minor party candidates have been able to amass the resources needed to wage campaigns that rival the efforts mounted by major party contenders.

Candidates for Congress do not receive public subsidies, but the FECA's contribution limits disadvantage minor party candidates for the House and Senate. These candidates can make unlimited contributions to their own campaigns, but are limited in the amounts they can accept from others. Individuals can contribute up to $1,000 and PACs can contribute up to $5,000 in each phase of the election—primary, runoff, and general. National, congressional, and state party campaign committees can each contribute up to $5,000 to individual House candidates in each stage of the election. State parties can give $5,000 to Senate candidates and a party's national organizations can contribute a combined total of $17,500.

Parties can also spend larger sums on behalf of candidates as "coordinated expenditures" that typically are given as polls, radio advertisements, television commercials, fund-raising events, direct-mail solicitations, or issue and opposition research (Herrnson 1988, ch. 3; 1995, ch. 4). Originally set at $10,000 each for a state and national committee, the limits for coordinated expenditures on behalf of House candidates are adjusted for inflation and reached $30,910 per committee in 1996.[3] The coordinated expenditure limits for Senate elections vary by state population and are also indexed to inflation. In 1996, they ranged from $61,820 per committee in the smallest states to $1.41 million per committee in California. The coordinated expenditure limits for presidential elections are also based on population; they reached $11.9 million in 1996.

Parties can also make other kinds of expenditures on behalf of their federal candidates. Since the FECA was amended in 1979, parties have been allowed to use soft money (which is raised and spent outside of the federal election system) on party-building activities, voter mobilization drives, and generic party-focused campaign advertisements that are intended to benefit their entire ticket.[4]

In addition, several Supreme Court rulings that were handed down in the midst of the 1996 election cycle made it permissible for parties to make unlimited expenditures on behalf of their candidates as long as they did not expressly advocate a candidate's election or defeat, or they were made independently of the candidate's campaign and without its knowledge or consent.[5]

One of the major effects of the FECA's matching funds, contribution, and expenditure provisions is that they leave minor party congressional and presidential candidates starved for resources. Few individuals or PACs are willing to invest in minor party candidacies, and those willing to make such investments give only limited amounts. Moreover, most minor parties, especially new ones, lack the funds to match the expenditures made by the two major parties. Campaign finance laws make it difficult for minor parties to compete in federal elections.

The mass media, while not considered a formal political institution, are an important part of the strategic environment in which candidates campaign. Positive media coverage can improve a candidate's name recognition and credibility, whereas negative coverage or an absence of press attention can undermine a candidate's prospects. Many major party candidates complain about the media, but virtually all of them are treated better than their minor party counterparts. Minor party candidates receive less coverage because the media are preoccupied with the horse-race aspects of elections, focusing most of their attention on the probable victors—usually Democrats and Republicans—

and ignoring others (Clarke and Evans 1983, 60–62; Graber 1993, 262–70).

Sometimes the media are openly hostile to minor parties. The press has historically been hostile to third-party candidates, and the coverage afforded to the New Alliance party, the Socialist Workers party, and other contemporary minor parties is often distorted and rarely favorable (e.g., Goodwyn 1978, 210; Schmidt 1960; Rosenstone et al. 1984, 90–91, 133–34, 229–33). A *Washington Post* article that appeared in the paper's style section in September 1996 illustrates the kind of ridicule to which minor party candidates are often subjected. The article, titled "There's the Ticket . . . A Selection of Running Mates for Ross Perot," listed Binti, the gorilla who rescued a toddler who had fallen into her cage, first. Also listed were Prince Charles of Great Britain and Jack Kevorkian, known as "Doctor Death" because of his involvement in physician-assisted suicides (*Washington Post* 1996).

The anti–minor party bias of the American election system stands in sharp contrast to the electoral institutions in other countries. Multimember, proportional representation systems, such as those used in most other democracies, virtually guarantee at least some legislative seats to any party—no matter how small, transient, or geographically confined—that wins a threshold of votes. Public funding provisions and government-subsidized broadcast time ensure that minor parties have a reasonable amount of campaign resources at their disposal (Nassmacher 1993, 239–44). All of these factors give the media incentives to provide significant and respectful coverage to many minor parties and their candidates. American political institutions buttress a two-party system, whereas political institutions in other democracies support multiparty systems.

Behavioral Underpinnings

Institutional impediments are not the only hurdles that must be cleared in order for minor parties to survive. Partisan identification and voting cues may have declined in importance during the past few decades, but most voters continue to identify with one of the two major parties (Keith et al. 1992, 17–23). Most voters' socialization to politics encourages them to consider minor parties outside the mainstream and unworthy of support. Some voters refuse to support minor party candidates for this reason or because of the outright hostility with which their campaigns are treated by the press. Others recognize that casting a ballot for a minor party candidate could contribute to the election of the major party candidate that they least prefer (Brams 1978, ch. 1; Riker 1982).

The relative ideological homogeneity of the electorate also deprives minor parties of bases of support that exist in more ideologically heterogeneous nations. Trying to outflank the major parties by occupying a place to the far left or the far right of the political spectrum rarely succeeds because Americans' moderate views do little to provide extremist parties with bases of support. The fact that the vast majority of Americans hold opinions that are close to the center of a fairly narrow ideological spectrum means that most elections, particularly those for the presidency, are primarily contests to capture the middle ground. At their very essence, Democratic strategies involve piecing together a coalition of moderates and voters on the left, and Republican strategies dictate holding their party's conservative base while reaching out for the support of voters at the center. Democracies whose voters have a broader array of ideological perspectives, or have higher levels of class or ethnic consciousness, generally provide more fertile ground for minor party efforts.

The career paths of the politically ambitious are extremely important in explaining the weakness and short-term existence of most minor party movements in the United States. Budding politicians learn early in their careers that the Democratic and Republican parties can provide them with useful contacts, expertise, financial assistance, and an orderly path of entry into electoral politics. Minor parties and independent candidacies simply do not offer most of these benefits. As a result, the two parties tend to attract the most talented among those interested in a career in public service. A large part of the parties' hegemony can be attributed to their advantages in candidate recruitment.

Voters are able to discern differences in the talents and levels of experience of minor party and major party candidates and, not surprisingly, they hesitate to cast votes for less qualified minor party contestants. As fluctuations in the support that minor party candidates register in public opinion polls demonstrate, even voters who declare their support for a minor party or independent contestant early in the campaign season often balk at casting their ballot for one of these candidates on election day. Major party candidates and their supporters prey upon Americans' desire to go with a winner—or at least affect the election outcome—when they discourage citizens from "throwing away their votes" on fringe candidates.

Mainstream politicians also respond to minor parties by trying to delegitimize their efforts. Major party officials have subjected minor parties to court challenges to keep them off the ballot. Major party nominees have often refused to debate minor party candidates. The 1992 presidential debates, which featured Perot, were the exception to the rule in that they included an independent. It is more common for minor party and independent contestants to be denied a place on the podium, as was Perot in 1996 and the nominees of the Libertarian party, the Natural Law party, and the nearly twenty other minor party and independent candidates who contested the 1992 or 1996 presidential elections. Major party nominees prefer to label minor party candidates as extremists and cast them as irrelevant in order to minimize their influence.

When a minor party or independent candidate introduces an issue that proves to be popular, Democratic and Republican leaders are quick to co-opt it. Perot proclaimed himself to be an agent of change and campaigned to cut the deficit and reform the political process. When these issues became popular many major party candidates, including then President George Bush and Democratic nominee Bill Clinton, staked out similar positions. By adopting positions espoused in popular movements, party leaders are able to better represent their followers, expand their constituencies, and attract votes (Eldersveld 1982, 40–43). Strategic adjustments that rob minor party and independent movements of their platforms are common in American history. They enable the two major parties to absorb, protest, and help maintain the existence of the two-party system.

Minor Party Forays

Despite the hurdles they must jump, a variety of minor parties have participated in the electoral process. Some have occupied an extreme position on the ideological spectrum, while others have tried to carve out a niche in the center. Some have taken stances on a wide array of issues, but others have mobilized around only one or two causes. Most minor parties have sought to elect presidential candidates, but some have focused on the state and local levels, and others have been more concerned with raising issues than electing candidates. A few have endorsed and even formally nominated candidates that have already won major party nominations. Some minor parties have survived for decades, but many last only one election. Minor parties can be classified using a variety of schemes (e.g., Key 1964, ch. 10). The scheme that follows divides them into four groups: minor parties that resemble major parties in their endurance and activities, those that form primarily around a single candidate, those that revolve around one or a small number of related issues, and those that survive largely by playing a supporting role for major party candidates.

Enduring Comprehensive Parties

Many of the minor parties resembled the major parties of their time (Rosenstone et al. 1984, 78–80). These parties were united by issues or an ideology and put forward candidates for Congress, the presidency, and state and local offices. They held contested nominations and selected their presidential candidates at conventions. They also employed campaign strategies and tactics that were similar to those used by the two major parties: they framed issues and adopted slogans that would help them secure their base and attract new voters; they used their resources to mobilize specific voting blocs whose support was necessary for electoral success. Moreover, they lasted for several elections. A few contemporary minor parties, such as the Libertarian party, founded in 1971, are similar to their predecessors in that they bear a resemblance to the major parties of their time (Hazlett 1992; Flood and Mayer 1996, 313–16).

During the nineteenth century, several enduring comprehensive parties enjoyed significant electoral success. The American (or Know-Nothing) party won control of the Massachusetts governorship and both chambers of the state legislature in 1854. Like its major party counterparts, and other successful minor parties, it used its control of the government to reward supporters with patronage and government contracts (Rosenstone et al. 1984, 57). Those minor parties that were in a position to distribute patronage and influence public policy usually survived for more than one election. The Greenback, Populist, and several other nineteenth-century minor parties lasted for over a decade.

Their extended presence on the political scene and their organizational strength made these parties attractive vehicles for politicians who wished to bolt from a major party. Politicians who were denied a major party nomination or found themselves unable to influence the party platform could advance their causes by joining an existing minor party. Former Whig President Millard Fillmore pursued this route of influence when he accepted the American party's presidential nomination in 1856, as did Tennessee Senator John Bell, who left the Whig party to become the Constitutional Union party's standard-bearer in 1860.

Contemporary enduring comprehensive parties, most notably the Libertarian party, rarely recruit candidates from the two dominant parties. Their weak political organizations, ideological extremism, and lack of electoral success reduce the attractiveness of these parties to successful major party politicians. Their inability to distribute political favors and limited influence over public policy have prevented these parties from amassing large followings and caused their number to dwindle. These parties have been largely replaced by less enduring candidate-focused parties.

Candidate-Focused Parties

Many of the minor parties that left their mark on the twentieth-century political landscape were highly candidate-centered. The same legal, technological, and cultural changes that influenced the development of the two major parties helped to shape the nature of their minor party contemporaries. The rise of the participatory primary, the enactment of the FECA, the introduction of polling, the electronic media, and modern marketing techniques into the political arena, and the decline of partisanship in the electorate helped foster the emergence of candidate-centered elections (e.g., Sorauf 1980).

Under the candidate-centered system, campaigns revolve around individual candidates, not parties. Elections are characterized by self-recruited candidates who field professionally staffed, money-driven campaign organizations that are not dependent on party workers. The two major parties play important supporting roles in the candidate-centered system, as do most twentieth-century minor parties (Herrnson 1988, chs. 3–4; 1995, ch. 4). However, the major parties enjoy an existence that is independent of and extends beyond their individual candidates' campaigns, whereas most candidate-focused minor party movements are merely extensions of individual candidates. They live and die with their candidates' campaigns.

The Progressive party, which was an offshoot of the Republican party, exemplifies modern candidate-focused minor parties. The Progressive party was constructed by former Republican Theodore Roosevelt after the tumultuous 1912 Republican Convention for the purpose of challenging his successor, William Howard Taft (Sundquist 1973, 164; Pinchot 1958, 172, 226–27). Roosevelt opposed Taft for the Republican nomination because Taft failed to continue his predecessor's battle to curb the power of corporate barons and improve the lives of ordinary workers. After losing the nomination to Taft, Roosevelt and his followers bolted the GOP and formed the Progressive party to mount Roosevelt's general election campaign.

Because it was a splinter group that drew its votes mainly from the progressive faction of the GOP, the Progressive party contributed to Taft's defeat at the hands of Democratic candidate Woodrow Wilson. Following the election, the Progressives failed to maintain a permanent organization or expand their efforts. In 1916, after extensive negotiations with Republican leaders, Roosevelt decided to return to the Republican fold. Many Progressives followed him, leading to the party's demise (Pinchot 1958, 226–27).

The Progressive party differed from the minor parties that preceded it in that it was little more than a vehicle for an individual politician (Rosenstone et al. 1984, 82). Previous minor parties had been built around causes, nominated candidates, and then waged their campaigns. The Progressive party drastically changed this pattern: it was organized for the purpose of campaigning for a preordained candidate.

A number of other minor parties were organized to promote individual candidacies. They included a new Progressive party that was formed in 1924 to support the presidential candidacy of former Republican Governor and Senator Robert M. La Follette of Wisconsin and the Union party that was organized in 1936 to promote the presidential candidacy of Republican House member William Lemke of North Dakota. These parties were all short-lived, disintegrating after their candidates lost the election (Rosenstone et al. 1984, 96, 101–02, 108–10).

The presidential candidacies of Democratic Senator Eugene McCarthy in 1976 and Republican Representative John Anderson in 1980 were conducted without the pretense of a minor party. These individuals were self-selected candidates, who assembled their own political organizations and mounted independent campaigns. They made little effort to ally their campaigns with those of candidates for lower office and their organizations were dismantled after the election was held.

Wealthy businessman Ross Perot's 1992 United We Stand America (UWSA) campaign bore many similarities to McCarthy's and Anderson's efforts. However, the Perot campaign differed in that the candidate was able to spend sufficient funds—$60 million—to mount a credible campaign. Perot's effort also differed in that after the election Perot transformed his independent candidacy into a new political party.

Recent events indicate that the new Reform party will probably fit the model of a short-lived candidate-focused party rather than become an enduring comprehensive party. First, Perot's money is the overwhelming source of the party's funds. Perot invested roughly $6.7 million to transform UWSA into the Reform party (Baker 1996a). Second, the party's nomination process appears to have been designed to provide a coronation for Perot rather than to select a nominee from among competing aspirants. In the first step of the process, each voter who signed a Reform party petition was supposed to be sent a nomination ballot that included the names of Perot, other self-declared candidates, and a place for a write-in candidate. In the second step, each candidate who received more than 10 percent of the nomination ballots—only Perot and former Colorado Governor Richard Lamm qualified—was given the opportunity to speak at the first Reform party convention. In the third step, a second set of ballots was sent to Reform party petition-signers, who were instructed to vote for Perot or Lamm by mail, telephone, or e-mail. In the final step, party officials announced the results of the second round of balloting and designated the party's nominee at a second Reform party convention (Greenblatt 1996).

News reports and the complaints of Perot's opponent indicate that the process may have been well planned for attracting media coverage, but it was poorly planned for the conduct of a competitive nominating contest. The balloting process was not well planned or executed. Many petition-signers received their ballots late. Others, including such prominent Reform party members as Lamm and Michael Farris, chairman of the California Reform party, never received a ballot. Still others received several ballots (Greenblatt 1996). Perot's influence over the process partially stems from his financing the party, including paying the firm hired to count the ballots. Moreover, flawed balloting procedures and a lack of interest among Reform party petition-signers resulted in only 43,057 returning first-round ballots and only 49,266 returning second-round ballots. Less than 5 percent of the petitioners participated in either round of balloting (Babbington 1996).

The nomination process also denied Lamm the opportunity to compete on a level playing field. Lamm's request for access to the list of petition-signers was refused by party officials, depriving him of one of the few means available to communicate with Reform party supporters.[6] Perot was the only Reform party candidate who had access to the party's supporter list, and he benefited from a direct-mail piece that featured his but not Lamm's picture (Fisher 1996). Another major avenue for communicating with petition-signers—a televised one-on-one debate—was never planned. Lamm's opportunities to communicate directly with party supporters were largely limited to speeches he gave at the party's state conventions in Florida and Maine.

The Reform party's decision to stack the deck so heavily in favor of Perot suggests that it will have difficulty making the transition from a movement dominated by a single charismatic leader to an enduring comprehensive party. This transition would require the party to develop a formal governing body that is independent of Perot, an independent source of financing, and a routinized system of candidate selection. It would also require the party to nominate candidates for state, local, and congressional office and to develop a permanent organization capable of assisting its candidates with their general election campaigns.[7]

It is more than likely that the Reform party will fold once Perot loses interest in politics and withdraws his financial backing. Perot's decision not to help other Reform party candidates on the ticket—he failed to appear with or endorse any of them (Baker 1996b)—did little to help their campaigns or to generate the kind of grassroots support that would be needed to enable the party to continue to build after it failed to achieve any significant success in the 1996 contest.

Single-Issue Parties

The source of strength for most single-issue parties (sometimes called ideological parties) is a salient, often highly charged cause or related set of causes. These parties differ from candidate-centered and enduring comprehensive minor parties, and from the two major parties, in that they are more concerned with advancing their issue positions than winning elections. Elections are typically viewed as an opportunity to raise public awareness for a party's cause, influence the political debate and the issue positions of major party contenders, raise funds, and recruit new members. Single-issue parties are often considered successful when they are able to get one or both of the major parties to adopt their core policy positions and enact those positions into law. Ironically, it is precisely that success that usually leads to a single-issue party's demise. Deprived of the core issue that unites it, the party frequently lapses into decline.

The Green party and the New York Right-to-Life party are examples of single-issue parties. The Green party grew out of the environmental movement that swept through the United States and Western Europe in the 1980s and 1990s. The party takes positions on a broad array of environmental concerns, including recycling, ecological economics, toxic wastes, energy, and organic farming. In addition to the environmental issues that form its doctrinal core, the party maintains positions on social justice, international, and political reform issues (Green Party of California 1996).

The Green party has enjoyed a degree of electoral success. Following the 1994 elections, twenty-nine Green party officials held elective office in ten states. During the 1996 election cycle, the Green party selected renowned consumer advocate and environmentalist Ralph Nader to be its presidential nominee. Although Nader won less than 1 percent of the popular vote, the fact that his name appeared on the ballot in twenty-two states helped to elevate the Greens' visibility and ensure that environmental issues would be discussed in the election. The campaigns that the party has waged on environmental initiatives and referendums have helped to raise its visibility and increase support for its goals, particularly in California—home of the strongest Green party state committee.

Unlike most contemporary parties the Green party has maintained a strong grassroots activist agenda. It continues to carry out local projects aimed at cleaning up the environment and educating citizens about pollution control, recycling, and other environmental issues. Literature circulated by the California Green party emphasizes that community projects and grassroots activities form one of the party's "two legs."

The Right-to-Life party also grew out of a social movement, but it has maintained a narrower focus than the Green party. Although the antiabortion movement has national foundations, the Right-to-Life party has had little impact beyond New York's borders. The party ran token campaigns for the presidency in 1976 and 1980, but as the next section shows, most of its influence has been through the cross-endorsements it has given to major party candidates running for office in New York State.

Fusion Parties

A fourth type of minor party—the fusion or alliance party—conducts many of the same activities as the two major parties and some of its minor party brethren, but differs in that it actively supports other parties' candidates. Some fusion parties can be categorized as comprehensive enduring minor parties, while others fit into the single-issue category. What makes these parties unique is that they engage in a practice known as "cross-endorsement," which enables a candidate to appear on more than one party's line on the ballot (Gillespie 1993, 255). Presidential candidate William Jennings Bryan, for example, appeared on more than one party's ballot in 1896 when he received the nomination of both the Democratic and the Populist parties. Fusion candidacies, such as Bryan's, became rare with the introduction of the Australian ballot. When they began printing ballots, many states enacted prohibitions against a candidate's name appearing more than once in the same contest. During the 1990s, ten states allowed a candidate's name to appear on more than one ballot line. Most fusion candidacies take place in New York.

New York has historically been the home of several fusion parties, most notably the Liberal, Conservative, and Right-to-Life parties. These parties resemble major parties and some minor parties in that they are enduring, have formal organizations, hold conventions, and attract volunteers and activists (e.g., Gillespie 1993, 258, 260). The Liberal party was founded in 1944, the Conservative party in 1962, and the Right-to-Life party in 1970. New York's fusion parties also resemble major parties in that they run local, state, and congressional candidates under their own label. Where they differ is that they routinely give their nominations to candidates who have been nominated by the two major parties and occasionally endorse each other's nominees. Most of New York's state legislators are elected on fusion tickets. The same is true of the state's congressional delegation. Of the fifty-seven major party candidates who ran for Congress in 1994, thirty-six were cross-endorsed by one of New York's minor parties. Both of New York's senators were also recipients of minor party cross-endorsements: Daniel Patrick Moynihan ran on both the Democratic and Liberal party lines and Alfonse D'Amato received the Republican, Conservative, and Right-to-Life nominations.

Fusion parties play important supporting roles to the major parties. They provide major party candidates with endorsements and grassroots campaign assistance. More importantly, fusion parties provide candidates with an extra place on the ballot that can be used to capture independent-minded voters who object to casting a ballot for a major party. This extra ballot line can also function as a safeguard for candidates who are unpopular with party activists. Republican incumbent John Lindsay, for example, was able to win the 1969 New York City mayoral contest after being defeated in the GOP primary because his name also appeared on the Liberal line of the general election ballot.

New York's fusion parties receive both material and policy benefits from their efforts (e.g., Gillespie 1993, 256, 259). They extract patronage from major party candidates in exchange for granting the candidates the opportunity to occupy their party's line on the ballot. They also influence the issues stances that are adopted by the major party candidates who seek their endorsements. The Liberal party pushes the candidates it endorses to the left, the Conservative party pushes them to the right, and the Right-to-Life party requires them to campaign on the party's antiabortion position. Ironically, a fusion party that succeeds in influencing the positions adopted by major party candidates can undercut its own constituent base.

Fusion parties do not automatically support the parties that are closest to them on the ideological spectrum. This occasionally causes the parties' endorsement strategies to backfire. In 1980, the Liberal party nominated incumbent Republican Senator Jacob Javits. After Javits lost the GOP nomination to Town of Hempstead Supervisor Alfonse D'Amato, his, D'Amato's, and Democratic nominee Elizabeth Holtzman's names all appeared on the general election ballot. Holtzman and Javits split the liberal vote, enabling D'Amato, who was the most conservative of the three candidates, to win. Given that most states ban fusion candidacies, it is likely that fusion parties, and the complications they sometimes cause, will continue to remain isolated to a few states.

Conditions for Strong Minor Party Performances

Support for minor parties ebbs and flows in response to national conditions, the performance of the two major parties, and the efforts of minor parties themselves. Minor parties usually attract more support under conditions of economic adversity, particularly when the agricultural sector is suffering. Minor parties also do well when the two major parties fail to address salient issues or when they nominate unappealing candidates (Mazmanian 1974; Rosenstone et al. 1984, ch. 5; Abramson 1995). As dissatisfaction with the major parties increases, minor parties increase in strength and number (Ranney and Kendall 1956, 458).

Minor parties can directly help their own causes by nominating popular candidates, particularly those who have previously held public office. Theodore Roosevelt, who occupied the White House as a Republican from 1901 to 1907, was the most successful of all minor party presidential candidates when in 1912, as the Progressive party nominee, he garnered 27.4 percent of the popular vote and 88 Electoral College votes. Former Democratic President Martin Van Buren, former Republican Senator Robert La Follette, and former Democratic Governor of Alabama George Wallace each picked up over 10 percent of the popular vote when they ran as minor party candidates for president. La Follette and Wallace also picked up significant Electoral College votes.

Of course, attractive minor party candidacies, national conditions, major party failures, and minor party successes are systemically related to one another. Celebrity candidates are strategic. They are most likely to run on a minor party ticket when their prospects for success are greatest—that is, when voters are dissatisfied with the performance of government, the incumbent president is unpopular, the two major parties have difficulty containing internal dissent or fail to adequately address the major issues, and one of the major parties did poorly in the previous election. The candidacies of these individuals, in turn, add to their party's ability to win votes (Rosenstone et al. 1984, ch. 6).

Systemic factors related to the emergence of the candidate-centered system have contributed to voter support for minor parties in the latter half of the twentieth century. The unraveling of the New Deal coalition and the rise of issue-oriented voting have weakened voter identification with the Democratic and Republican parties, which has benefited their minor party opponents. The transition from a grassroots, volunteer-based style of campaigning to a high-tech, money-driven style also may have worked to the advantage of minor parties. Parties and candidates that can afford to purchase polls, direct mail, television and radio advertisements, and the services of professional campaign consultants are no longer penalized by their lack of volunteers and party activists.

These conditions, the nature of their constituencies, and their prior political records made important contributions to Lowell Weicker's successful gubernatorial campaign in Connecticut and Bernard Sanders's ability to win election to Congress from Vermont.

The Historic Roles of Minor Parties

Minor parties have historically performed many of the same functions as the major parties. They provide symbols for citizen identification and loyalty, educate and mobilize voters, select and campaign for candidates for office, aggregate and articulate interests, raise issues, advocate and help to formulate public policies, organize the government, provide loyal opposition, institutionalize political conflict, and foster political stability. As their relative status indicates, minor parties tend to be less adept at performing many of these roles than are their major party counterparts.

Minor parties also play four additional roles that are important to the functioning of the political system: they raise issues that have been ignored by the two major parties, serve as vehicles for voters to express their discontent with the two major parties, help propel the transition from one party era to another, and occasionally act as laboratories for political innovation. Minor parties have raised issues that have been ignored or inadequately addressed by the major parties during many key junctures in American history (Sundquist 1983). The Free Soil and Liberty parties took important stands on slavery prior to the Civil War. The National Women's, Equal Rights, Prohibition, Greenback, Populist, and Socialist parties and the Progressive party of 1912 advocated female suffrage (Gillespie 1993, 284). More recently, the Green party has raised environmental concerns to new heights. In the first example, minor parties propelled the formation of a new political party—the modern Republican party. In the second two, they forced the major parties to confront significant issues, and in one case this resulted in an amendment to the Constitution. In all three examples minor parties made it possible for a variety of groups and issues to be better represented in the political process.

In providing outlets for protest, minor parties function as safety valves that channel societal frustrations into mainstream forums. Minor parties institutionalize conflict by championing the causes of alienated voters and encouraging them to express their dissatisfaction at the polls rather than in the streets. The Populist, Progressive, and Socialist Workers parties, for example, have harnessed the anger of some of the poorer elements of society. This anger might have otherwise been directed toward overthrowing the political system. During the 1990s,

Perot's minor party movement gave alienated and apathetic voters who were turned off by the major party nominees a way to register their displeasure without resorting to violence.

The regularity with which minor party forays precede political realignments indicates how they help to redefine the political cleavages that divide the major parties. By raising new issues and loosening the ties that bind voters to the major parties, minor parties promote political realignments (Freie 1982; Burnham 1970; Sundquist 1983). The efforts of the Free Soil, Liberty, and other pre–Civil War minor parties hastened the development of the modern GOP and the third party era. The Populist party's efforts to expand the money supply helped usher in the fourth party system. The campaign waged by the La Follette Progressives helped pave the way for Franklin D. Roosevelt and the Democrats to expand the role of the federal government. Perhaps Perot's UWSA campaign and Reform party efforts will some day be interpreted as precursors to a sixth party system that is structured around deficit-related issues.

Another role that has been historically performed by minor parties is concerned more with political processes than public policy. Because minor parties are born and die with some frequency, they are important sources of political experimentation and innovation. In 1831, the National Republican party introduced a major innovation in the presidential selection process when it held the first national nominating convention (Ranney 1975, 16). During the 1990s, Perot's minor party movement capitalized on modern technology and voters' desires for direct political involvement when it aired the first televised infomercial and held the first national presidential primary. If voter response to these innovations is favorable, they may some day be adopted by one or both of the major parties.

Conclusion

For most of its history, the United States has maintained a two-party system. This system has been shored up by the nation's political institutions and the activities of voters, the media, politicians, and the two parties themselves. Nevertheless, minor parties have raised critical issues, provided outlets for frustrated voters, and helped realign the nation's politics at key points in history. They have also introduced innovations into the political process. Minor parties have played, and continue to play, important roles in the American two-party system.

Notes

1. The Constitution provides that when no candidate wins a majority of the Electoral College votes, the election is to be decided in the House of Representatives.
2. Once they qualify for federal funding, major and minor party candidates lose their eligibility for additional public funds if they win less than 10 percent of the vote in two consecutive primaries in which they compete. Candidates that lose their eligibility can requalify for public funds by winning at least 20 percent of the vote in a subsequent primary.
3. Coordinated expenditure limits for states with only one House member were set at $61,820 per committee in 1996.
4. Soft money is considered largely outside of federal law and is subject to the limits imposed by state laws (e.g., Alexander and Corrado 1995, ch. 6; Biersack 1994).
5. The most important of these are *Massachusetts Citizens for Life v. Federal Election Commission*, 479 U.S. 238 (1986) and *Colorado Republican Federal Campaign Committee v. Federal Election Commission*, U.S., 64 U.S.L.2 4663 (1996).
6. Party officials claimed that making the list available would violate federal election laws.
7. The party nominated and elected a few candidates for local office in 1995 in a small number of states and it endorsed some congressional contestants in 1996. However, the numbers who were nominated are too small to classify it as an enduring, comprehensive minor party.

2

The Impact of New Parties on Party Systems: Lessons for America from European Multiparty Systems

Robert Harmel

In the 1960s, political scientists Seymour Martin Lipset and Stein Rokkan (1967) suggested that party systems had been essentially *frozen* since the 1920s, and argued that they were likely to remain that way for the foreseeable future. By "frozen," they meant not only that the major parties were likely to remain the same, as were the bases of support within the electorate for various parties, but also that the party actors would go largely unchanged. There would presumably be few new parties, or at least few that would have much impact on their systems.

Nevertheless, new parties of all varieties have been added to established party systems since the 1960s. Much has been written about new ecology parties with a leftist tendency, as well as new parties of the extreme and often anti-immigrant right. In the United States, the Greens, the Natural Law party, the Libertarians, and Ross Perot's Reform party have all gained some attention during recent elections. At least 91 completely new parties (excluding another 112 resulting from splits or mergers) were added to 15 established European competitive party systems between 1960 and 1980 alone. Twenty-five naturally formed new parties were added to the American party system during that same period.

This chapter is about new parties and the extent to which they make a difference. It is based on the premise that it is possible to learn a lot about one's own political institutions by comparing them to counterparts in other countries. A number of important lessons can be learned by comparing and contrasting American new parties with the experiences of new parties in Europe, including countries with very different electoral and party arrangements. First I describe the situation in Europe and then I draw lessons for American parties.

How New Parties Can Make a Difference

The alleged effects of new political parties range all the way from destabilizing their party systems to reinvigorating those systems. By definition, *all* competitive parties are interested in winning some governmental positions. But most parties are motivated by more than just the desire to win positions for their own sake; they are also (and in some cases more so) concerned with affecting governmental policy. Indeed, the average party has many goals, and different parties may have different primary goals, but nearly all new parties want to win some legislative seats or affect policy in some way. The greatest probability of making an impact on policy rests with those parties that actually have some electoral success and differ from established parties on the issues.

Three related questions are useful for assessing the impact of new parties:

1. To what extent are new parties in Europe electorally successful?
2. To the extent that some are successful, do those tend to be parties that offer a difference or just an echo of what established parties are offering?
3. Aside from what new parties can accomplish by being in governmental positions themselves, is there evidence that new parties also affect policy by getting established parties to change their positions?

New Parties' Electoral Success and Government Participation

For European new parties, some minimal level of electoral success is not only important in its own right, it can also be critical to the party's chances of influencing the system in other ways, such as affecting coalition arrangements, getting other parties to change their positions on important issues, or even shifting the nature of political debate.[1] Hence, the picture of widespread electoral failure presented in the second column of table 2.1, with the large majority of the European new parties lacking *any* electoral success and only one in four "breaking through" to representation in parliament, would seem to bode poorly for new party impacts overall.[2] That picture is somewhat misleading, however.

Although most European countries have fully proportional election systems (where legislative seats are distributed to parties roughly according to percentages of votes won), Britain and France do not, and neither did West Germany. With electoral systems that set higher the

Table 2.1
Electoral Success of Naturally Formed New Parties

Success Score[1]	Fifteen European Countries	Germany[2]	France and United Kingdom[3]	Twelve European Countries[4]
0	69.0	94.1	75.0	46.3
1	3.4	5.9	8.3	—
4	20.7	—	16.7	39.0
5	2.3	—	—	4.9
6	4.6	—	—	9.8
	100.0	100.0	100.0	100.0
(N)	(87)	(34)	(12)	(41)

1. Success scale:
   0 = 0.0–1.0% of vote;
   1 = 1.01–4.99%;
   2 = 5.00–10.00%;
   3 = more than 10% but no seats;
   4 = up to 10% of seats;
   5 = more than 10% of seats;
   6 = participation in cabinet.
   Each party was assigned its maximum success score for elections during the period from party birth through 1994.
2. "Mixed" election system.
3. "Plurality/majority" systems.
4. Proportional representation systems.

hurdle for gaining seats (as is true also in the United States),[3] those three countries account for a greatly disproportionate share of unsuccessful new parties in western Europe, as is evident in the third and fourth columns of table 2.1. Although the electoral structures of England, France, and particularly Germany have apparently not constrained the *formation* of new parties, it is clear that the achievement of *electoral success* has been far less likely within such structures (Harmel and Robertson 1985).

When the new parties of England, France, and Germany are removed from the analysis—as they will be from now on—the rate for winning seats in the remaining twelve countries jumps to slightly over 50 percent. Equally interesting, of course, is the fact that nearly half have never received more than 1 percent of the vote nor any seats. Even in systems of proportional representation, it is far from certain that a new party will succeed in achieving even "small party" status. Political effects that require the new party to be perceived as an electoral threat by other parties would seem to be beyond the reach of a large proportion of new parties in Western Europe.

New Parties on the Issues: A Difference or an Echo?

Do European new parties significantly differ on the issues from their more established counterparts? If not, they may still offer different personnel or different organizational styles or strategies. However, all other things being equal, new parties that merely echo the positions of others have less potential for affecting government policy than parties that offer a difference on the issues.

A new party may bring something new to its system's issue profile in two different ways. First, it may occupy a different position from all existing parties along the dominant cleavage dimension of the system, which for the systems considered here is the left–right dimension. An example would be a new party with extreme right-wing positions in a system where no such party existed previously. Second, a new party may develop and promote a new issue that is not associated directly with the left–right continuum, and that is not clearly addressed by other established parties. Ecology parties would have been obvious examples in many countries in the 1970s and 1980s.

In this regard, Thomas Rochon (1985) has distinguished between two types of new parties, *mobilizing* parties and *challenging* parties. While mobilizing parties seek to mobilize voters on some new issue cleavage, challenging parties are content to challenge existing parties on their own turf for an already mobilized part of the electorate. It is helpful to think of new parties as actually fitting into four categories:

- A *left–right challenger* is a party that takes its place at a position along the left–right continuum that is already occupied by another party.
- The *new issue mobilizer* comes closest to Rochon's use of the term "mobilizer." This party does not fall on the traditional left–right cleavage, but instead seeks to mobilize voters over some "new" issue.
- A *left–right mobilizer* seeks to mobilize new voters or entice experienced voters to a previously unoccupied position on the left–right continuum.
- *Other issue* parties constitute a residual category of parties that fall off the left–right continuum, but that are not primarily con-

cerned with "new issues." (Included among the *other issue* parties are those developed primarily to promote regional concerns.)

By comparing each new party's positions to those of its system's parties prior to 1960, it was possible to determine which new parties fit in each of the four categories.[4]

As reported in the first column of table 2.2, 54 percent of the naturally formed new parties could be placed on the left–right continuum, with three-fifths of those parties located in occupied positions as left–right challengers, and the remainder taking unoccupied positions as left–right mobilizers. New issue mobilizers account for less than one in five of the new European parties of the 1960s and 1970s.

Challengers versus Mobilizers: Which Are More Successful?

Are the parties "with a difference" among the parties that have at least some electoral success?

Table 2.2
Frequency and Success of Naturally Formed New Parties in Proportional Representation Systems, by Type of Party

Party Type and Category	% of Total	% of Total with Success	Success Rate[1]	Mean Success Score[2]	(N)
All Challengers	0.32	0.27	0.46	2.00	(13)
of Micro Party	0.15	0.14	0.50	2.34	(6)
of Large Party	0.17	0.14	0.43	1.71	(7)
Left-Right Mobilizers	0.22	0.32	0.78	3.33	(9)
New Issue Mobilizers	0.17	0.14	0.43	2.00	(7)
Other Issue Parties	0.29	0.27	0.50	2.33	(12)
	(41)	(22)			

1. "Success rate" is the percentage of parties in the category who have had success in obtaining at least one seat in parliament.
2. See table 2.1 for definition of success score.

Rochon has argued for doubting that mobilizers will be as success-ful—or at least as successful *as quickly*—as challenger parties because mobilizing a party's own electorate is a more difficult task than "steal-ing" (or at least "borrowing") from another party's already mobilized electorate. On the other hand, successful mobilizers may be expected to survive longer than challengers because "It is much harder for an established party to coopt a new political cleavage than it is for that party to destroy a challenger by adjusting its program within the con-fines of its current alignment" (Rochon 1985, 419–40). From Rochon's argument, it may be inferred that mobilizers should take longer than challengers to become successful electorally, and that mobilizers may in fact be less likely to break through at all. Those mobilizers that do eventually become electorally successful should, however, endure longer than challengers.

Since party deaths are not as frequently or accurately reported as party births, it is not possible to address Rochon's expectation regard-ing long-term durability. However, we can say something about his first two propositions. From the perspective of Rochon's thesis, the results of table 2.2 (columns 3 and 4) are mixed at best. Contrary to expecta-tions, left–right mobilizers have actually been somewhat *more* likely than challengers to achieve representation, and the new issue mobi-lizers have had the same average success score as that of challengers. It is also noteworthy that—again contrary to expectations—the suc-cessful mobilizers have been nearly as likely as challengers to have broken through in their first attempts, though it is true that none of the new issue mobilizers have done so.

As for change in electoral fortunes over time, the general story is one of stability. Few of the new parties have clear trends either up or down in support over time (considering only those parties that experi-enced four or more elections through 1994). Only three have done markedly better over time; supporting Rochon's thesis, two were new issue mobilizers and the third a left–right mobilizer. Additionally, it is not only challengers of large parties who have done relatively poorly compared to left–right mobilizers. New parties that have challenged "micro" parties have done only slightly better than direct challengers of more successful established parties.

Findings from the Cross-National Comparison

What patterns are apparent in the experiences of the new parties of established Western European democracies with multiparty systems? First, it has been possible for new parties working within proportional electoral systems to win representation in their national legislatures. Through 1994, approximately half of the new parties born between 1960 and 1980 have done so.

Second, parties that offer a difference on the issues have been able to achieve some electoral success. The new parties that offer a difference on the traditional cleavage dimension actually have a better record of electoral success than parties that offer an echo. Even the parties offering the greatest choice (i.e., the new issue mobilizers) have been nearly as successful as the left–right challengers. In fact, among the five new parties with the greatest success in winning seats are representatives of two relatively new trends in European politics: ecology parties (Belgium's Ecolo and Agalev) and far right-wing, antiestablishment parties (Denmark's and Norway's Progress parties). Third, although most of the new parties have experienced little change in support over time, mobilizer parties have been more likely than challengers to grow in electoral strength over time.

Thus far we have focused on the ability of European new parties to achieve some level of electoral success. This concern presumes that votes or seats are preconditions for affecting politics in other ways. In order to bring about a major change in the nature of political debate or to become a viable coalition partner, for instance, a new party will certainly need to become (or at least demonstrate the potential to become) a significant player in elections and in the parliament. And votes in parliament are also essential for a party that is not equipped— whether in profile, in temperament, and/or in motivation—for participation in government, but which instead pursues a direct impact on policy through effective use of legislative "Blackmail!" (Sartori 1976).

A third strategy for affecting government policy is much less direct, and is especially relevant to parties which offer a new choice on the issues. A new party may hope to have an impact on policy by causing another party to adopt—or at least move toward—its positions (Downs 1957, 127, 131). In an effort to identify some factors in successfully implementing this approach in multiparty systems, we turn next to examination of two illustrative cases from Scandinavia.

Impacts on Old Parties' Issue Positions[5]

The original raison d'être for some new parties is not to win offices for itself so much as to impact policy indirectly through influence on larger, more established parties' issue positions. As Anthony Downs has argued, even though all party founders hope to win some votes and seats eventually, "some parties—founded by perfectly rational men—

are meant to be threats to other parties and not means of gaining immediate power or prestige" (Downs 1957, 127–128).

But, as Downs also notes, getting another party to change its identity is no easy matter:

> Ideological *immobility* is characteristic of every responsible party, be-
> cause it cannot repudiate its past actions unless some radical change in
> conditions justifies this. . . . Once more uncertainty is the decisive factor,
> because it may prevent the party from knowing what policies are most
> appropriate. In the absence of this knowledge, responsibility makes it
> ideologically immobile. (1957, 110–11)

In an earlier study, Lars Svåsand and I argued that because of the
tendency of parties to follow an "if it isn't broke, don't fix it" approach, "just being there" would not be sufficient for new parties to
influence their older competitors.

> But to the extent that the new kid on the block could reduce its older
> neighbor's uncertainty as to what is the right move, change could in fact
> result. (Harmel and Svåsand 1997, 316)

And one way of reducing the uncertainty would be for the new party
to establish itself as a direct *threat* to the older party's electoral well-
being. The threat should be most apparent, we thought, when the new
party is doing well enough electorally to be noticed and the target party
is experiencing an electoral downturn attributable to the new party.

In search of support for our argument, we then drew upon the
experiences of two relatively new right-wing parties—the Progress
parties of Norway and Denmark—and their established Conservative
party neighbors. The two Progress parties shared many features and
circumstances, including original purpose: to entice the Conservatives
back to the right by effectively challenging "the establishment." Both
parties became identified with and by their quixotic founders and were
assigned something of a "pariah" status by the established parties
whom they intentionally maligned. However, their situations also differed in some potentially important ways, including how well the Conservative parties were performing electorally and how strong the
Conservatives were relative to the parties of the center.

Using the parties' platform positions to measure policy orientation,
we carefully examined and coded both Progress parties' and both Conservative parties' positions on nine issues that were closely associated
with the identities and original purposes of the Progress parties, including personal taxes, governmental scope, and regulation of the private
sector. This was done for each of the parties' platforms from the early

1970s through the early 1990s. We determined that both Conservative parties had moved somewhat to the right since development of the Progress parties, though the Norwegian party had changed even "more substantially and a bit more consistently" than its Danish counterpart. The Norwegian Conservatives also moved very quickly on some of the issues, without waiting to see whether Progress would last.

Some aspects of these findings were surprising. Although both Progress parties won impressive parliamentary seats during their first elections in 1973, it was the Danish Progress party whose first election was of earthshaking proportions. It won twenty-eight seats and nearly 16 percent of the vote, compared to the Norwegians' four seats and 5 percent of the vote. And while the Danish Conservatives lost dramatically when Progress debuted (dropping from thirty-one to sixteen seats), and only gradually recovered, the Norwegian Conservatives were able to maintain their twenty-nine seats and actually picked up strength after that. According to our argument, the Norwegian Conservatives had little reason to change dramatically, and they certainly should have been outdone by the Danes.

Did the behavior of the Norwegian Conservatives indicate that a new party could influence change in its neighboring party's platform simply "by being there," even without demonstrating significant prowess as a direct electoral threat? We think not. Instead, our hypothesis had failed to recognize two aspects of parties' character that were now apparent: "They not only can see parties on two sides of them at once, but they can also presumably look to the future as well as the recent past" (Harmel and Svåsand 1997, 337).

The Norwegian Conservatives could move to the right without much to fear from a declining group of center parties, whereas the Danish party could not move rightward without worrying that a healthy set of nonsocialist rivals might take advantage of the situation. So while the Danish Conservative party was somewhat constrained in the actions that it could take in adjusting to what was clearly a new threat on its right, the Norwegian party was free to pursue a kill, thereby eliminating what it may well have seen as a *potentially* significant threat (which had, after all, won some seats in its very first election).

If the Norwegian Conservatives adjusted their issue positions to eliminate the Progress threat, the move has not been successful. Although Progress lost all of its seats in its second election in 1977, it again won representation in 1981 and 1985, and then experienced its own triumphal election in 1989, winning twenty-two seats on 13 percent of the vote. In Denmark—where the Conservative response came more slowly and less dramatically—the Progress party has never gone unrepresented in the Folketin (parliament), though its wins in the 1980s and early 1990s were less impressive than those in the 1970s.

Despite succeeding electorally at a level that most new parties can only dream about, it is highly unlikely that either Progress party will lead a government. In fact, until quite recently, the other nonsocialist parties would not even consider including the Progress parties in future coalitions. Nevertheless, in both cases the new Progress parties—encouraged and aided by important changes in the social structures of their countries—posed significant immediate or potential threats to the major parties on their immediate left and thereby influenced those important parties to alter their platforms. In so doing, each of these new parties has already affected the nature of the choices provided in its party system, and has potentially affected the policy behavior of governments that include the Conservatives. Each has successfully implemented the strategy of its founder: to potentially affect policy by getting established parties to change their positions. The relevance of these experiences for American new parties will become clear in the following paragraphs.

Lessons for the American Parties

The American party system is often described as unique, and as such, there would seemingly be little to learn from comparison to European parties. Given the well-known, very important differences between the dynamics of two-party and multiparty systems, and between the constraints imposed on small parties by the associated plurality and proportional representation electoral systems, there may at the outset seem to be little mutual relevance for new parties in those two types of systems. But despite the important differences, there are a number of "lessons" that can be meaningfully drawn from comparing the situation of new parties in the United States with the experiences of new parties in Europe.

First, the American party system is not unique in its propensity for forming new parties (or perhaps more to the point, for any supposed propensity *not* to form new parties). Although some might assume that the unwelcoming nature of plurality elections would keep new parties from forming, the United States has been among the most prolific of the established democracies in forming new parties. The experiences of Britain, France, and the former West Germany provide additional evidence that while certain electoral systems may hamper the *electoral success* of new parties, they apparently do not discourage their *formation.*

Second, the most important lesson to be learned by comparing the two-party and multiparty systems is that different election systems have produced different expectations regarding new parties' chances for electoral success and governmental participation. Whereas it is not unreasonable for a new party operating within proportional representation to hope for votes, parliamentary seats, and even executive office (normally as part of a governing coalition), the realistic naturally formed new party operating under America's plurality rules would hope only for enough votes to be noticed.[6] Although proportional representation is often combined with a minimum threshold for participation in parliament, those thresholds are much less forbidding than the requirement of gaining a plurality.

Indeed, twenty-two of the forty-one naturally formed new parties in countries with proportional representation had broken through to parliamentary representation. Although most of those parties have won only small numbers of seats in given elections, the fact is that small numbers of seats can often make a big difference in multiparty arrangements, especially at the time of coalition formation. The few seats held by a new player may in some circumstances (1) render irrelevant some coalition arrangements that would otherwise be viable, (2) make the new party itself a viable coalition partner, or (3) give the new party "blackmail potential" with which to influence government from the outside. As an example of the latter potential, the Norwegian Progress party's two parliamentary votes were needed to keep a bourgeois government in power in the mid-1980s, and when that government proposed an increase in the petrol duty, Progress withdrew its support and effectively brought down the government. If the other nonsocialist parties had underestimated the Progress party's resolve to oppose tax increases, it is not likely that the same mistake would be made in future bourgeois governments. As evidence that new parties can reasonably aspire to government in Europe, four of the naturally formed new parties included in this study have participated in coalition governments. In the United States during the same period, no new party won even a single seat in Congress.

If new parties are not formed with the expectation of winning an executive office or even parliamentary seats, then what is their purpose in systems where such expectations would be unrealistic? Elsewhere, John Robertson and I have distinguished between "contender" and "promoter" parties. Contender parties are "those having the perception that they can be, at least eventually, electorally successful," while promoter parties are "those that may recognize the unlikelihood of winning many votes or seats, but whose major objective is to use the party as a vehicle for bringing attention to a particular issue or cause"

(Harmel and Robertson 1985, 517). The observation that most American new parties are of the promoter variety is hardly new; the realization that such parties are far from unique to this country may not be so commonly understood. Forming new parties in the absence of much hope for electoral success is not even limited to the other countries with nonproportional representative election systems. In just the proportional representative systems of Western Europe nearly half of the new parties formed naturally between 1960 and 1980 had never won a seat—nor more than 1 percent of the votes in parliamentary elections—through 1994.[7]

Despite a high probability of electoral failure—in all types of election systems—new political parties continue to be formed. Although it is doubtful that there is only one motivation behind formation of all such parties, it is likely that issue *promotion* is a major factor in many. Benjamin Bubar, a leader of the older Prohibition party in the United States, may have expressed this thinking of his new-party counterparts when explaining his party's presidential campaign in 1976:

> We've got some issues that need to be discussed. It gave us a springboard. We have a political message that we think America needs. We're not going to the White House, and we may not win, but we're having an impact. (Quoted in Smallwood 1983, 43)

Attracting attention to themselves and their cause is apparently the raison d'être of such "minor parties."

This is not to suggest, of course, that votes and seats are irrelevant to the promotion of causes or issues. Rare indeed are the parties that see electoral success as a hindrance rather than a means to achieving their policy objectives. Even those content to be promoter parties must recognize a relationship between attention paid to a new party—by other parties or the media—and its likelihood of making a difference in elections or in government. As argued above, it is important for a new party seeking policy impact—especially if that impact is to be won indirectly through influence on another party's positions—to demonstrate enough electoral prowess to affect (or potentially affect) the target party's own seat count. In multiparty systems, where even just winning enough *votes* to alter the other parties' seat distribution would certainly garner attention, the currency of choice is normally seats themselves rather than votes. With relatively small amounts of that currency, new ecology parties of the left and antiestablishment parties of the right (including Norway's Progress party in its early years) affected not only specific positions taken by other parties, but in some cases the content of political discussion more generally. Lest new parties in the United States take too much heart from the feats accomplished with so few seats, it must be emphasized that *some* seats were involved in each case.

In the context of an electorate and an electoral system that very seldom reward a minor party with even one seat in Congress, American new parties have only votes with which to threaten the Democratic and Republican parties. And hampered by the "wasted vote" phenomenon, minor parties find it difficult to obtain—let alone sustain—even enough votes to be perceived as much of a threat. Although the most successful American new parties of the past included some well-documented splits from major parties, the most successful new parties recently have been formed naturally.[8]

George Wallace's American Independent party was a left–right mobilizer (located to the right of the Republicans) in 1968. The Libertarians, arguably a new issue mobilizer, have not been so successful in national races, but have won offices in local races since being founded in 1971. The fact that both parties, especially the American Independents, were founded to offer a difference on the issues is not inconsistent with our findings for Europe. And that the American Independents could find support to the right of the Republicans, who may have gradually moved closer to the center and the Democrats over time, is not inconsistent with earlier arguments by Downs concerning the likely placement of "influence parties" (1957, 131). That something similar would also happen in the multiparty systems of Denmark and Norway, though, would actually contradict Downs's expectations that influence parties would be found "almost exclusively" in two-party systems, since "Party ideologies are relatively immobile in multiparty systems" (1957, 131–134). The lesson here seems to be that new parties with a difference—especially if the difference is on the dominant cleavage dimension of the party system—can aspire to change other parties' positions, whether those new parties exist in the hostile electoral environment of the plurality system or in a multiparty system where target parties are often "ideologically constrained" by viable competitors on both sides.[9]

Of course, one would be remiss not to mention Perot's relatively successful candidacies in 1992 and 1996. Although Perot did not develop a formal party organization until after the 1992 election, the phenomenon of which he was a part resembled in many ways the early development of the Danish and Norwegian Progress parties. In all three cases, the main orientation was antiestablishment. In none of the three were specific policy stances particularly clear to those who first gave voting support. And in the Scandinavian countries, as in the American case, the new "movements" were founded by and clearly identified with "interesting characters," who used television to good effect. Danish tax lawyer Mogens Glistrup was widely known for his appearance on a talk show during tax preparation season, when he had called upon his countrymen to avoid paying taxes by all available means, and likened tax evaders to resistance fighters during World War II. Norwegian dog kennel owner Anders Lange attracted attention to himself and his new party by what could only be described as bizarre behavior, which included wearing a sword at a nationally televised debate. And while Perot's behavior may have been ordinary by comparison, there is no denying that his unconventional speech and demeanor helped attract attention on talk shows such as *Larry King Live.*

Given that both of the Progress parties have sustained some support and developed more normal party organizations over nearly a quarter of a century now, should this be seen as boding well for the future of the new Reform party? It is true that both Progress parties have developed more positive—and less exclusively protest-oriented—agendas over time and that both have survived transitions to a second generation (in the Danish case, a third generation) of leadership. But it is also true that in both cases, the party leaders were not the only members elected to positions in parliament. Parliamentary groups are likely to demand *normal* party organization with routinized procedures and have the potential for developing alternative leadership. In the United States, where it is difficult for third parties to win votes for president but nearly impossible to win seats in Congress, it is much less likely that "one-person" presidential parties such as the Reform party can be sustained beyond the loss of interest by, or in, the party's founder. Hence, in the United States even more so than in the multiparty systems, the personality-based identity that can at first attract attention and votes to a new party may also be the seed of its destruction.

In summary, the experiences of American new parties are not as unique as sometimes alleged. New parties are just as numerous here as elsewhere, and the purposes and circumstances of American new parties bear similarities to at least some new parties in the multiparty systems of Western Europe. Yet it is impossible to escape the conclusion that when compared to their counterparts in multiparty systems abroad, America's new parties are severely handicapped in the ways by which they can influence politics and limited in the degree to which they can do so. Whether the main culprit is the plurality electoral system or a society that accepts and even prefers that system, the result is the same. New parties in the United States—regardless of location or strategy—cannot reasonably aspire to executive office nor are they likely to win even one seat in Congress. Without the perks and the "threat potential" of elective positions, such parties are limited not only in their aspirations, but also in what they can contribute to their democracy. Unless and until the society becomes so dissatisfied with the status quo that it demands electoral proportionality, American new parties will likely be limited to promoting issues or policy positions, even as they go through the motions of contending for office. While some of their European counterparts represent and a few even govern, American new parties can hope only to influence.

Notes

This chapter draws heavily upon a number of earlier papers, some of which are coauthored I especially owe debts of gratitude to Lars Svåsand and John D. Robertson for allowing me to use ideas and words that were originally developed jointly. While acknowledging the considerable contribution of Lars and John, I accept sole responsibility for any errors of fact or interpretation.

1. New parties' potential impacts, and how those are affected by electoral success, are discussed more thoroughly in Harmel and Svåsand (1990).

2. Most of the data on which table 2.1 is based were originally collected by John Robertson and me in 1983–84, though the data set has since been revised to incorporate a number of corrections.

3. These three systems lack full proportionality but differ in important ways. Britain's system is a first-past-the-post plurality system. Germany's is a mixed system that allows voters to cast two ballots, one for an individual and the other for a party list. The individual candidate elections are decided by plurality, while the party list election is proportional. In addition, a German party is not awarded any of the seats decided by proportionality unless it has won three direct seats or 5 percent of the national vote, a scheme designed to make it difficult for small parties to win seats. France has a two-ballot, majority system where candidates with less than 12.5 percent of the vote on the first ballot are automatically eliminated. Some small parties have been more successful than others in negotiating deals between ballots, sometimes resulting in seats from the second, plurality-based ballot. (France did have proportional representation in 1986.) Generally, Britain is considered a 2 or 2½ party system, Germany a 2½, and France a 3½ party system.

4. A ten-point ideological scale was adopted from *Encyclopedia Britannica Book of the Year,* which facilitates comparisons to parties in the previous systems, whose ideological positions were already coded on this scale by the *Book of the Year.*

5. This portion of the chapter draws heavily from previous work by Robert Harmel and Lars Svåsand, some of which is reported in Harmel and Svåsand (1997).

6. There are some new minor parties with seats in the European countries with plurality/majority systems, of course, but most of those involve products of splits or mergers.

7. Some of those parties may have won something at a more local level, but it is likely that most have not.

8. Among the most successful "new parties" of the past have been the Populists in 1892 (naturally-formed; won 8 percent of presidential vote and 22 electoral votes), the Bull Moose party of 1912 (a Republican split; won 27 percent of vote and 88 electoral votes for Teddy Roosevelt), the Progressives of 1924 (arguably a naturally formed

party; won 17 percent of vote and 13 electoral votes). Though not doing as well in the national vote due to a limited regional base, the Dixiecrat split from the Democrats in 1948 resulted in just 2 percent of the vote but 39 electoral votes for Strom Thurmond.

9. It should be noted that Downs's argument regarding influence parties in two-party systems referred to parties to the "outside" of a major party, as opposed to parties formed between the two main players. In both the Danish and Norwegian cases discussed above, the Progress parties were also formed in unoccupied territory to the right of what was previously the most right-wing political party. More centrist parties in multiparty systems, hemmed in by existing parties on both sides, would probably find it more difficult to alter their positions than the Conservative parties, who had not faced viable opposition from their right for some time and who in fact were accused by some supporters of having moved toward the center over time.

3

The Case for a Multiparty System

Kay Lawson

The United States has a multiparty system. There are always many parties that manage to get on some of the ballots some of the time, and in the 1996 presidential election minor parties took 10 percent of the popular vote (*Ballot Access News* 1997). The United States does not have a two-party system, but rather a "bi-hegemonic" one, where control of almost all the elective posts rests in the hands of the elected representatives of two major parties. There are numerous minor parties, some enduring, some not, and all with very minor influence indeed.

The argument of this chapter is not that multipartyism should be introduced in the United States, but rather that it should be strengthened and encouraged. This argument is divided in three parts: why true multipartyism is preferable to bi-hegemonism, what changes would permit its expansion, and what steps are currently being taken in this direction. In passing I will argue that many of the ills Americans are accustomed to blaming on multipartyism are owed to other factors, factors whose negative effects can be exacerbated by multipartyism, but need not be.

Why Multipartyism Is Preferable

The most powerful argument for multipartyism is that it is more *natural*. Political parties are formed by those who seek to control government offices for their own purposes. Those purposes may be selfish or civic-minded, good or evil, intelligently or stupidly conceived. All we can say for sure is that in the absence of restraints there will be a very great number of purposes around which office-seekers will form parties. The new states of Eastern and Central Europe made this point very clear: 80 parties competed in the 1992 Czechoslovakian elections and the same year there were 131 parties in Poland (Schmidt 1992).

More recently, 47 parties and 25,000 candidates registered for the elections in Bosnia in September 1996 in pursuit of 42 seats in the House of Representatives and a three-member national presidency. There were thus more parties than there were offices available and among them they produced an average of 555.5 candidates per office (Bonnar 1996). If it were *easy* to get a new party on the ballot and wage a meaningful campaign, no doubt the United States could do better than Bosnia.

If, then, it is natural to have many parties, there must be very good reasons for passing laws that discourage parties so drastically as to produce just two capable of waging effective campaigns for office. There are, of course, many things that are "natural" yet are nevertheless restricted for the common good. But extreme restrictions on our basic freedoms of speech and association are always unwelcome, and are acceptable only when deemed absolutely essential for important aspects of our common good. It is often argued that restricting our political parties to two helps us achieve the reconciliation of diverse interests, moderation, and consensus. This is not in fact true (see below), but even if it were, these are not the kinds of goals for which a democracy sets aside its freedoms. Diversity of opinion is recognized not only as a normal by-product of political freedom, but also as a fruitful source of innovation and progress. Achieving moderation and consensus while reconciling diverse interests is desirable, but is not worth the sacrifice of fundamental freedoms.

Besides the advantage of protecting that which is natural in a free society, encouraging multipartyism offers two more positive rewards: it offers greater protection of minority rights and it enhances majority rule. No one doubts that a multiparty system offers ideological, racial, ethnic, or other minorities a better chance than a bi-hegemonic system does of electing some representatives to legislative bodies. Elected representatives, even when constituting only a small minority in a legislature, have greater opportunity to be heard than the same people outside the government.

More controversial is the claim that a multiparty system is also better than a bi-hegemonic system at producing majority rule. To make this point clear, it is necessary to distinguish between "producing majority rule" and "producing a governing majority." Producing majority rule means that a majority of the eligible electorate has effective say over national policy. Producing a governing majority means simply that more than 50 percent of the elected members of government have sufficient agreement to pursue a shared program. Of course, majority rule includes the formation of a governing majority. But it means more than that. It means that the members of the governing majority will normally be in agreement not only with each other, but also with majority views *in the nation* on most issues. This is the definition of majority rule that we commonly associate with the definition of democracy. However, a *governing* majority can exist among elected officials, and indeed more and more commonly does exist, which is very remote from any *national* majority of the electorate.

To demonstrate that a multiparty system is better at producing majority rule, we must first ask how good two-party systems are at the same task. As Maurice Duverger (1959) taught us and as others have demonstrated (Downs 1957; Lijphart 1977, 1984), the principal cause of bi-hegemonic party systems is the existence of a single-member, single-ballot plurality electoral system. Such a system gives the advantage to the two parties that are strongest and rapidly marginalizes or eliminates the others. This situation is not antimajoritarian at its inception: normally the two top parties become the strongest *because* they are the most likely to win a majority in any given election. Such a system, when first established, is thus a good way to move toward majority rule, so long as everyone takes part.

However, this early and no doubt deserved advantage can then be used by the two strongest parties to maintain their grip on power *even when they no longer have the loyalty and support of a majority. The effect of the single-member plurality system is not the same over time. The advantage the leading parties have can be made to outlast their own majoritarianism.* This situation develops because, once in power, the elected representatives can—and do—manipulate the laws governing the electoral process to their advantage and against weaker parties. Examples include laws governing ballot access, internal party operations, and campaign finance (see chapter 11). Under these circumstances, successful minor party challenges are all but impossible.

Thus, even when the two strongest parties have declined precipitously in the voters' affections, and neither is any longer truly majoritarian, the legal regime keeps minor parties from organizing and offering alternatives to the voters. The poor showing of minor parties in such a system cannot be dismissed on the grounds that they simply do not interest the voters; the scales have been tipped against them before they ever formed and certainly before they can wage an effective campaign.

Furthermore, a bi-hegemonic system is antithetical to majoritarianism because it is not necessary for either party to win a majority of the eligible votes, but simply a majority of the votes cast. The leaders of the major parties in a bi-hegemonic system quickly learn that it is a waste of time and money to campaign for the votes of habitual nonvoters. This situation obtains in the United States today, where the major

parties are not even *seeking* a majority of the eligible electorate.[1] One
or the other of the major parties will stay in power even when voting
rates drop precipitously, even when the president and the ruling party
in Congress are both elected by less than 25 percent of the eligible
electorate (as in 1994 and 1996). All each party needs is to get more
votes than the other major party.

Having no serious competition besides each other, the leaders of
such parties are free to become more and more minoritarian, and they
do not even have to pay much attention to the wishes of a majority of
their own best supporters. Bob Dole was not the first newly nominated
presidential candidate to say he agreed with "some" of his own party's
just formulated program—that was Jimmy Carter, in 1976.

Thus, if democracy means rule by the majority of the eligible electorate, bi-hegemonic systems do not foster democracy. However, there
are those who would argue that democratic majority rule is achieved
whenever free elections produce a governing majority. Yet despite all
the folklore to the contrary, it is far from clear that a system in which
two parties dominate so heavily is better at producing even that kind
of majority. There are only two significant bi-hegemonic party systems
in the world: the United States and Great Britain.[2] The U.S. system is
not noted for producing a strong governing majority. It far more often
produces government stalemated by the conflicts between two governing majorities, one in Congress and one in the presidency. The British
parliamentary system, also with single-member districts and election
by plurality, does routinely produce a strong governing majority within
Parliament. Although the ability of the majority to accomplish its announced purposes is dubious (Rose 1984), we may count the British
system as a bihegemonic system that ensures a governing majority.
That makes one.

In contrast, multiparty systems can and often do produce a strong
governing majority and true majority rule. In multiparty systems everyone—or almost everyone—can find a party to support. Except for
Switzerland, a very special case in which multiparty rule is constitu-
tionally guaranteed by a collective presidency, voter turnout in European multiparty systems is always well above 50 percent (and is
normally in the eighties and nineties). There are, of course, other factors affecting turnout; the crucial point is that in these systems those
who vote do so in support of a wide range of parties, programs and
points of view, and know they may have reasonable hopes of electing
at least a few representatives to office who share their opinions.

Furthermore, multiparty systems are better able to bring that national majority into the governing process. In a multiparty system
smaller parties that represent numerically significant minorities are

likely to succeed in placing some of their members in legislative office. Such members may have views on certain issues that permit them to join and strengthen the majority in government. Or they may be in close enough agreement with other parties, major and minor, to help form a governing majority that is far more representative of the majority views of the public than would result from the mere giving over of governance to the victorious party in a two-party system.

Of course, some of the parties in a multiparty system are, inevitably, "extremist." Democracy requires that such opinions be heard and considered. An expanded multiparty system in the United States would give parties representing such points of view, on the left and on the right, a greater chance of representation in legislative bodies, state and national. But so long as such opinions are considered extreme, parties representing these points of view would not gain sufficient seats to control the national agenda. When such a party threatens to develop enough power to influence the direction of policy, it then behooves those who find its point of view repugnant to develop opposing arguments and educate the electorate. Seeking to escape the tougher challenges of democracy by denying fundamental freedoms has the result of seriously weakening democracy itself.

What about the case of a very small centrist party that can gain seemingly inordinate power by being the linchpin in successive governing coalitions with larger left- or right-wing parties (such as the Free Democratic party in Germany)? While rare, when such a situation occurs it is a sign that the national majority itself is strongly centrist; otherwise, the electorate would not continue to support both left- and right-wing parties willing to rule in tandem with such a centrist party. Once again, the burden falls on those who find such a condition repugnant to make a stronger case to the electorate; a system that protects the freedoms of a wide range of parties (as does the German system) ensures their opportunity to do so (cf. Lind 1992).

Do multiparty systems cause governmental instability? Parliamentary coalitions sometimes come apart, and either new elections must be called or various games of ministerial musical chairs must be played to reconstitute a majority. The fact is, however, that short of revolution or coups d'état, governments fall only when the cabinet loses the support of a majority in the lower house, or when the chief executive calls for new elections in pursuit of a new majority that is now believed to exist. The motives for forcing the fall of a government are often complex, sometimes venal, but always linked to majoritarianism. The election (or the ministerial reshuffling) either reassures the government and the nation that the former majority is sustainable or puts the government into closer fit with the national majority by establishing a new governing majority.

In any case, it is not the existence of multipartyism that causes governments to fall. Governments fall in bi-hegemonic Britain. Parliamentary government is normally multipartisan, but the whole world is "normally multipartisan," including quasi-presidential France and the many developing nations that have adopted the French system of government. Furthermore, it is not necessarily an evil to have a system of government that encourages the strengthening of the link between the national and the governing majority whenever that link becomes dangerously weakened. But the key point here is that such a practice does not depend on how many parties a nation has, but rather on what kind of constitutional system it has.

It is possible for multipartyism in combination with other national conditions to produce serious fragmentation. However, there are fair and workable ways to ensure the continuing presence of a national majority behind a ruling party or coalition of parties, using methods that have been widely applied in contemporary Europe. What is required is careful tinkering with the electoral system—not to serve the interests of an entrenched minority and not in order to eliminate the rights of other minorities—but rather to find ways to combine the free and natural formation of parties with the *engineered* formation of a sufficient majority to make stable and effective government possible.

The most common way to achieve this end is to set a threshold for representation in the legislature—any and every party may get itself on the ballot, but only those receiving 5 percent or more of the national vote will have the right to seat a representative.[3] Another method is to have a certain portion of the seats of the legislature allotted to those elected in single-member constituencies (as in Germany, Spain, and Italy), and the rest of the seats allocated by proportional representation. In Germany, half of the 664 deputies to the Bundestag are elected in direct balloting within their respective constituencies, while the other half are selected proportionally from party lists of candidates in each of the Länder (states). Similarly, the Spanish senate is elected by simple plurality, but its lower house is elected by proportional representation. Italy now chooses 75 percent of its legislature by plurality voting, and 25 percent by proportional representation (Lijphart 1994; Zimmerman 1994). Such combinations of systems ensure that smaller parties will find it worthwhile to participate—some of their candidates will almost surely be elected—while strengthening the majority of the victorious party or coalition of parties.

A third way to ensure that fragmentation does not paralyze a multiparty system is to have two ballots, allowing anyone to participate on the first ballot, but eliminating from the second ballot all candidates with less than a certain percentage of the vote (12.5 percent in French legislative elections). The second vote is then won by a simple plurality. Or the second ballot may be limited to the two top contenders, as in the case of elections for the French presidency. In either case, the first ballot protects multipartyism and majoritarian voting (there were nine candidates on the ballot in the 1995 presidential election in France), and the second reduces the field and makes a cohesive governing majority more feasible.

A final way to encourage majoritarianism within a multiparty system is to exercise fair control over the quality of the campaign, and in particular to ensure that the campaign messages of all the parties have a roughly equal chance to be heard, regardless of the wealth of the organizations, the candidates, or their supporters. No other nation allows candidates to spend as much as in the United States. The argument that the imposition of spending limits is an unconstitutional infringement on free speech, but that the imposition of limits on contributions is not, makes no sense whatsoever. Where is the individual who has written a check for a candidate without spending money? What is the basis of an argument that spending money one way to influence election results is an expression of free speech and spending it another way is not? The decisions of the U.S. Supreme Court in *Buckley v. Valeo* (1978) and subsequent cases refusing to limit soft money spending are illogical and among the most deleterious the Court has ever imposed on our political system.

Spending limits are common throughout the rest of the democratic world, as are prohibitions against certain kinds of spending; for example, the French forbid all paid advertising. Combined with extensive public funding and the provision of free media time, such regulations produce a reasonably level playing field that invites all to play. Easy access to the broadcast media brings the parties into a shared arena, where debates with each other and with journalists permit the emergence of a national agenda. Minor parties have a chance to convince others that the key issues for their electorates belong on that broader agenda. The resultant election is far more likely to produce a genuine national mandate—and thus a more meaningful governing majority even if coalition government is required—than elections in which only two parties take part—and tacitly collude to keep the more uncomfortable issues out of debate (Kaid and Holtz-Bacha 1995).

Expanding Multipartyism in the United States

If a strong multiparty system is better than a bi-hegemonic one, what would it take to establish such a system in the United States? Five changes would be required. The first four would give minor parties a fairer chance in the United States.

First, all laws that discourage the formation of new parties or ballot access for minor party candidates should be abolished.

Second, public funding should be extended to all campaigns and should cover both candidate and party activities, with spending limited to that funding.

Third, private campaign donations, including a candidate's own money and that of interest groups, should be prohibited.

Fourth, access to the media should be free and generous, and commercial advertising should be prohibited.

Several of these changes represent a modest curtailment of individual freedom, but all have been accepted in other democracies as essential for the maintenance of a more important freedom: the right to take a meaningful part in one's nation's governance. None of them is designed to maintain the special privileges of an elite.

The fifth and most important change is more fundamental. The electoral system should be changed to the system used in most of the rest of the world: proportional representation (PR) with multimember districts and seats allocated according to each party's share of the vote, with a 5 percent threshold. Possibly some seats in legislatures should be reserved for representatives elected in single-member districts.

PR is clearly the electoral system most conducive to multipartyism and, as such, is an important step in moving away from bi-hegemonism and toward stronger multipartyism in the United States. Adopting PR will require major changes in election law. Under this system each district chooses several representatives, and each political party offers the voters a list of candidates for its posts. In some nations, such as Belgium, the voters can vary the order of the candidates on the list; in others, as in Switzerland, the voters have multiple votes that they may spread around as they wish among the lists. In the simplest and most common version, each voter casts one vote for one party list and the parties are then awarded seats according to the proportion of the vote they received. The exact distribution is determined by a formula, such as the "largest remainder system" or "the highest-average system" (*The Economist* 1993).

As noted above, in Germany, Italy, and Spain, PR is used in combination with single-member constituencies. It is used in unmixed form in Israel, Malta, most Latin American and former Soviet bloc nations, South Africa, and Cambridge, Massachusetts. New Zealand, Russia, Mexico, and Japan have recently adopted mixed systems with a component of proportional representation (*The Nation* 1996). In Europe only France and Britain do not use PR (but in the latter, the Labour party has promised a national referendum on the question if elected in 1997). The French system offers an alternative that would move in the same direction as PR, albeit less dramatically: single-member districts with runoff elections if no candidate wins a majority of the vote.

Whatever formula is used, minor parties with no chance of winning a plurality may well win a seat or two when PR is adopted, and will not necessarily feel pressured to drop out or to combine with other small parties just because they are not doing well—this remains true for numerous small parties even when a threshold of 5 percent of the vote is required to gain a seat (a limitation that does tend to eliminate the very smallest parties). Under such a system, the voters are given the maximum amount of choice consistent with producing a governing majority. The legislature (or council or board) is not only closely keyed to the actual vote but is also much more fully representative of all points of view.[4]

Prospects for Change

Are there any serious prospects that the United States will soon adopt any of these changes? Although the legal and cultural barriers against minor parties remain formidable, and were amply illustrated in 1996, two cases suggest that modest changes may be on the way: the Reform party's campaign for the presidency with candidate Ross Perot and the debate over the right to place a fusion ticket on the ballot.

In the case of the Reform party, media coverage made it clear that even when the party's leader is a billionaire, the present system works unreasonable hardships on a new party. Perot met the extremely difficult and varied criteria for ballot access in all fifty states. He made the politico-cultural judgment to use only public funds, supplemented generously by soft money expenditures on his behalf (which is of course what the major parties' candidates did as well), and his party shaped its convention and its nominating procedures to provide a closer fit to the national norm. Nevertheless, he was denied access to the presidential debates and was regularly denied the right to buy media time in the amounts and at the times he preferred. Although it is possible that Perot would not have done even as well as he did (8.5 percent of the vote) had he been treated more fairly, his campaign provided new evidence of the degree of difficulty a new party faces in seeking that access—access that would have been accorded automatically to such a party in every other modern democracy.[5]

The fusion ticket debate took on new importance during the 1996 campaign season. Fusion means that two or more parties agree to support a single candidate for an office; the ballot permits voters to indicate which party they support in choosing that candidate, and the tally of the vote shows clearly how much of a candidate's score he or she owes to the minor party. Fusion candidacies were fairly common practice in the United States throughout the nineteenth century but were widely banned thereafter. They are now illegal in forty states, and are common only in New York and Connecticut.

The reason most often given for banning fusion is that it helps avoid "voter confusion." Those who have studied the origin of antifusion laws are, however, convinced they were "passed to squelch minor parties" and that they have been successful in doing so. Furthermore, says Theodore Lowi, antifusion laws are patently unconstitutional limitations on political association: "It's no different from prohibiting parties from having overlapping programs. These laws . . . bar some parties from putting their chosen candidates on the ballot while granting that right to other parties" (Lowi 1996a).

The minor party most ardently pursuing the right to fusion is the New Party. Formed in 1992 as "a progressive coalition of union members, community activists, environmentalists and minority voters," it has chapters in ten states and branches in fifteen cities. Concentrating on local elections (school boards, city councils, and county boards), the New Party has endorsed candidates in 140 contests, of which 94 were successful. Many of these contests were officially nonpartisan, a legality the party seems to have cheerfully ignored.[6]

The New Party argues that fusion nominations allow a minor party not only to "signal its qualified support for a major party candidate" but also to demand some loyalty to its own values when its supporters make a telling contribution to electoral victory. It argues that this "is the *only* way for a minor party to be both principled and relevant" in elections where its own candidates have no chance of winning (Lowi 1996b). In 1994, the New Party challenged the Minnesota ruling against fusion tickets by nominating a state legislator who had already been chosen by the Democratic–Farmer–Labor party of Minnesota. The state ruled the nomination illegal, the party took its case to court, and in early 1996 the Eighth Circuit U.S. Court of Appeals declared that the prohibition was unconstitutional. The state appealed, and the case (now *Timmons et al. v. Twin Cities Area New Party*) was heard by the U.S. Supreme Court on December 4, 1996, at which time Chief Justice William H. Rehnquist pointed out to the attorney arguing for the New Party, "If we were to rule for you, it would result in quite sweeping changes in a great many states" (Greenhouse 1996b). Supporters of expanded multiparty politics heartily agree.

The tactics of other groups seeking to strengthen the role minor parties play in the U.S. system are similar to those employed by the New Party: wage the battle in circumstances where victories may possibly be gained; when possible, seek broader change through legislation or the courts. One such group is the Center for Voting and Democracy (CVD), led by founder Rob Richie and John Anderson, the former independent candidate for president. The CVD is not linked with any particular minor party. Its goal is to spread the use of proportional representation and thus to improve the chances of establishing multiparty democracy, with fairer representation of minorities and minority points of view. The CVD has established a "representation index" that measures the percentage of an eligible electorate who help elect a member to the lower house. Those who cast several votes in multimember districts clearly have a better chance of helping to elect at least one winner. In 1994, the U.S. index was 22 percent; in Germany with only partially proportional representation, it was 75 percent (Bleifuss 1995).

Like the New Party, the focus of the CVD is on elections to bodies that are already based on multimember districts: school boards and city councils. Instead of seeking to elect particular candidates, however, this organization seeks to persuade the district's electorate to shift to a system of proportional voting. In 1996 its most impressive advance was in San Francisco, where it succeeded in placing "preferential voting" for that city's Board of Supervisors on the ballot, and gaining 44 percent of the vote. Preferential voting is a form of proportional representation (PR) that was introduced in twenty-two cities during the Progressive era but voted out by all of them except Cambridge, Massachusetts before 1960, because, according to political scientist Kathleen Barber, "The old political leaders whose activities were curtailed by reform fought back to regain their power" (Bielski 1996, 10). It is still used in Ireland, Malta, and Senate elections in Australia. In this system, voters rank their choices for the seats available and if a voter's top candidate is eliminated, the ballot is transferred to the next highest ranked candidate, a system that its proponents claim "prevents communities of interest from splitting their vote among rival candidates . . . allows citizens to vote for their favorite candidates [and] promotes coalition building" (Hill and DeLeon 1996). The groups endorsing this form of PR in San Francisco ranged from the Police Officers Association to the San Francisco Democratic party to groups representing gays and lesbians, greens, seniors, Latinos, and Asians (*The Nation* 1996).

The CVD also joined the effort of Representative Cynthia McKinney (D-Georgia) who has introduced legislation (the Voters' Choice

Act) to overturn federal requirements that states use single-seat districts. The McKinney bill would permit states to establish multimember congressional districts in which legislators would be elected through one of three different proportional representation voting systems. McKinney's motives are not entirely impersonal: she was originally elected in a congressional district whose boundaries were based on race, a practice the Supreme Court ruled unconstitutional in early 1996. Rather than argue with the verdict, she has turned to PR as "a new approach giving all Americans the opportunity to have a voice in our halls of power" and although a change in the voting system could mean that some already elected black officials would face new opposition, her proposed legislation has drawn support from fellow members of the Congressional Black Caucus, as well as from the CVD and other groups (Bleifuss 1995).

Perhaps the most remarkable success of the CVD, however, has been in its ability to get its message into print. A by no means complete list of the newspapers and news magazines in which articles and editorials supporting the change to proportional representation have appeared, many of them written by officers of the group, includes the following: *Atlantic Monthly, Boston Globe, Chicago Tribune, Christian Science Monitor, Cincinnati Post, Dallas Morning News, The Nation, New York Times, New Yorker, San Francisco Chronicle, USA Today,* and *Washington Post.*

Conclusion

Is change imminent in the rules governing the American party system? Probably not. Even when seriously dissatisfied with the choices they are given, most voting Americans still support the bi-hegemonic system, while nonvoters, marginalized by the major parties and denied meaningful alternative choices, simply grow less interested in the political game. Neither group imagines that changing the rules of that game would make an important difference.

Yet the rules of the game do matter. Rules that permit and encourage multipartyism give more interesting alternatives to all the players and create a special invitation to those who have felt themselves forced out of the game to come back in. And the policy results are far from negligible. Strong multipartyism is the international norm, and while none of the countries that practice it are utopias, the performance of other developed nations in an array of public policy areas, including education, health care, public transportation, child care, care for the elderly, and programs combating homelessness, drug abuse and crime, is almost always far superior to that of the United States. None of these nations have the vast resources of natural wealth and military dominance that characterize the United States and all of them are faced with the same dilemmas of how to improve global economic competitiveness. How then do they do it? It seems reasonable to infer that the answer has something to do with the key difference between their political systems and our own. And that key difference is this: these nations protect the freedom of their citizens to form new parties and they provide an electoral arena in which all parties have an opportunity to make their case. The United States does not.

Notes

1. It is now standard procedure in the United States to campaign for the votes of the marginal voters, not wasting valuable resources on habitual nonvoters or on those with consistent voting patterns. According to Ganz (1994), the targeted population for a modern campaign will be as little as 22 to 27 percent of the total potential electorate and those not targeted "are far more likely to be of lower socioeconomic status. . . . They will never hear from a campaign and thus will likely stay at home on election day or vote the way they always have."

2. Jamaica has had a two-party system for over fifty years. However, the system has been marked by frequent periods of instability, particularly during the 1970s, and in 1993 the elected members of the opposition party refused to attend the sessions of parliament on the grounds that the election that year had been so marked by fraud and corruption as to be invalid (Wilson 1993).

3. It is sometimes argued that 5 percent is too high a figure for a new party. However, in the Netherlands, where a party needs only 0.67 percent of the total vote to gain a seat in the 150-member parliament, it can take up to six months to organize a governing majority after an election.

4. There appears to be a link between the election of women representatives and the use of PR, although this is a matter of dispute (Bleifuss 1995; Rule et. al. 1996).

5. Not every other democracy would have allowed the buying of media time, but none would have permitted such a ban to be unequally applied. Of the nine candidates presented to the French in the 1995 presidential elections, all of whom received sufficient free media time to ensure the electorate's familiarity with their programs and arguments, only three could have met the standard of "electability." No one imagined this was an adequate reason for denying access. The distaste television commentators felt for the person and arguments of far right candidate Jean-Marie Le Pen may have been constantly apparent on their faces, but was rigorously excluded from their language as well as from the determination of the amount of coverage such a candidate should receive.

6. Requiring that local elections be nonpartisan is an antiparty regulation that is found nowhere else in the world. Although challenged every now and then as patently unconstitutional, this requirement is quite common in U.S. towns and cities.

4

In Defense of the Two-Party System

John F. Bibby

As America prepares to enter a new millennium, the viability of its two-party system is being called into question on a number of fronts (Lowi 1996b). Ross Perot's winning 19 percent of the popular vote for president in 1992 and then succeeding in forming the Reform party which in 1996 qualified for the ballot in all fifty states and for public funding under the Federal Election Campaign Act (FECA) demonstrated considerable potential for well-financed independent candidacies or third parties. A poll in 1995 revealed that 63 percent of the citizenry supported the formation of a third political party that would run candidates for president, Congress, and state offices against Democratic and Republican candidates (*Washington Post* 1995, A11). In 1996, 76 percent of people polled said they thought Perot should be included in the presidential debates, even though the bipartisan commission on presidential debates barred Perot from participating on the grounds he had no reasonable chance of being elected. David Broder, the respected *Washington Post* correspondent, even went so far as to predict the demise of one or both of the two major parties unless they can solve the nation's looming entitlement crisis within eighteen months after the 1996 elections (1996, C1, C4).

Less apocalyptic are political scientists who specialize in the study of political parties. Even these specialists, who have a long tradition of commitment to parties as being essential to the democratic process, express concern about the current state of the parties as American politics becomes increasingly candidate-centered (Epstein 1986, 37–39).

Despite these and other indicators of stress in the two-party system, one of the hard facts of American politics has been the overwhelming electoral dominance exercised by the Democratic and Republican parties since the realignment of 1854–1860. Nowhere else in the world have the same two parties so completely and continuously dominated free elections. This suggests that two-party politics is highly compatible with American society, culture, and governmental structures. Other chapters in this volume clearly demonstrate how institutional arrangements (e.g., the Electoral College, single-member districts) work to perpetuate a two-party system from which the Republican and Democratic parties benefit. However, it is important to keep in mind that "no electoral system can protect major political parties from the electorate," as the Progressive Conservative party of Canada learned to its sorrow in October 1995 (Abramson, et al. 1995, 366–67). Furthermore, as the Republican party's displacement of the Whigs in 1854–60 demonstrated, a new party can overcome structural barriers by changing the nation's issue agenda. It is, of course, fortunate for the country, though unfortunate for third parties, that no issue as divisive as slavery has restructured American politics since the 1850s.

As the comments in the previous paragraph indicate, the basic argument presented in this chapter is that not only is the two-party system compatible with American society, it is also a highly positive force in American politics and continues to serve the nation well. It is certainly a stretch to assert that it is the two-party system that is somehow responsible for government's seeming inability to respond decisively and promptly to societal problems when the public is divided and unclear about the course it wants public policy to take in such critical issues as entitlement reform.

Providing Elected Officials with Legitimacy

The two-party system limits the real and meaningful choices of the electorate to either Republican or Democratic nominees in virtually all elections other than local and judicial contests. As a result, the election day winner is assured of having amassed either a majority or sizable plurality of the vote. This lends an aura of legitimacy to elected officials that in the case of the presidents and governors strengthens their position to lead the nation or their states.

In assessing the impact of the Electoral College system for electing presidents, Nelson W. Polsby and Aaron Wildavsky note quite candidly that "One of its hidden effects . . . is to restrict the number of parties contesting the presidency." But they go on to stress that

> This helps focus the electorate on a limited menu of choices. In turn, this increases the chance that winners will have the backing of a sizable number of voters and the legitimacy to lead Congress and the nation. (1996, 295)

They further note that one of the polity-fragmenting consequences of replacing the Electoral College with a direct popular vote system would be to create incentives for organized minorities to run candidates for the presidency in anticipation of a second, runoff election. A runoff would always be a possibility because advocates of direct popular vote believe that it is essential that the winner receive a substantial plurality of the popular vote (e.g., at least 40 percent of the popular vote was specified in the constitutional amendment approved by the House in 1969). Therefore, if no candidate meets the specified minimum percentage of the vote required for election, a runoff election between the top two finishers would be necessary (Polsby and Wildavsky 1996, 294). The 1992 election provides evidence that the need for runoff presidential elections forced by more than two parties seriously contesting for the presidency is not an imaginary possibility. With an unusually strong third-party candidate in the race in 1992, a fourth-party candidate would have needed to poll only 6 to 7 percent of the national popular vote to deny Bill Clinton even 40 percent of the vote. It is not hard to imagine candidates representing the religious right, right to life groups, African Americans, or environmentalists being able to muster 6 to 7 percent of the vote and force a runoff (Polsby and Wildavsky 1996, 294).

It should also be noted that the Electoral College system is not producing pernicious results. The research of Paul Abramson and his colleagues demonstrates in a convincing manner that neither George Wallace (1968), John Anderson (1980), nor Ross Perot (1992) could have won a head-to-head contest against either the Republican or Democratic presidential nominees (Abramson et al. 1995, 355–56).

America has many societal cleavages and minorities that hold the potential for a much more divisive politics than has yet been experienced. Fortunately, the two-party system (with encouragement from such devices as the Electoral College) creates incentives for various interest groups to compromise and work within the existing parties instead of fragmenting the political/governmental order with an array of separate parties each having distinctive followings and ideological doctrines to which they are committed. With just two parties having a reasonable chance of winning, compromises among groups are facilitated within parties, and the winning Democratic or Republican president is assured of a large enough share of the vote to enter the White House with a mantle of legitimacy that a system based upon the consent of the governed requires.

Encouraging National Unity, Reconciliation, and Policy Moderation

Critics of the American two-party system are wont to fault the Democratic and Republican parties for failing to provide clear-cut policy alternatives to the voters and for too often running "me too" campaigns. It is also asserted that a multiparty system would provide voters with a range of policy alternatives that is now lacking in the existing system. Instead of complaining about a system dominated by two moderate and centrist parties, we ought to be thankful that a wide variety of diverse American citizens can be accommodated by these two parties. As Willmore Kendall and Austin Ranney observed, a variety of social forces and characteristics operate to minimize the "civil-war" potential of American society. But they stress that "it is the party system, more than any other American institution, that consciously, actively, and directly nurtures consensus" by drawing its leaders, workers, and candidates from all strata of society, appealing to voters broadly rather than to narrow interests, and promising most groups some but not all of what they seek (1956, 509). Given the diversity within society, the parties cannot ignore the constellation of groups in American political life if they are to have any hope of achieving elective office (Keefe 1994, 67).

Because candidate recruitment and political advancement in the United States are primarily through the two major parties, the likelihood of demagogues and extremist candidates either winning major party nominations or being elected is reduced. Both the Democratic and Republican parties have broad-based electoral support and draw significant levels of support from virtually every major socioeconomic group in society (blacks are an important exception with their overwhelming support for the Democrats). These parties dare not risk alienating important elements of society and must maintain their credibility with the voters to remain viable. These considerations operate against extremist candidates garnering either major party nominations or party organizational support in primaries or general elections. In those rare instances in which demagogues have secured major party nominations, leaders have normally condemned these candidacies and thereby prevented them from being elected and in the process protected the party's integrity (e.g., the GOP leadership's abandonment of Ku Klux Klan leader David Duke when he won the primary to become the Republican nominee for governor of Louisiana in 1991).

In today's highly charged atmosphere of talk radio, single-issue groups, heightened ideological awareness, political action committees, and attack ads, John Fischer's 1948 observation about the crucial consensus-building role of America's two major parties is perhaps more valid than ever. He noted that

> The purpose of European parties is, of course, to *divide* men of different
> ideologies into coherent and disciplined organizations. The historic role

of the American party, on the other hand, is not to divide but *unite*. (Emphasis added, 1948, 32)

Only once in American history has the two-party system failed in its duty to achieve national reconciliation and consensus and then "to the astonishment of each side, the North and South found themselves at war" (Brogan 1954, 513).

Perhaps it is because the United States has operated a political system within the context of stability, consensus, and incremental policy change for so long that its advantages tend to be overlooked and taken for granted. It does, however, strike one as passing strange that some should be looking to replace a two-party system that has been so successful in "trying to discover some way of bringing together into a reasonably harmonious relationship as large a proportion of the voters as possible" (Herring 1940, 102) with a multiparty system that would in all likelihood further fragment society and heighten divisiveness.

As V. O. Key Jr., the post–World War II era's leading student of American political parties, has observed, the tug of each party's durable foundation of electoral support tends to fix fundamental policy orientations of the two major parties. Yet the diverse makeup of each party restrains the zeal of the party leadership in the advocacy of the cause of any one element within the party. Thus the composition of the parties and the need to expand electoral support to independents and disaffected members of the opposition will moderate the outlook of the parties' leadership and their candidates (Key 1964, 219–20). Witness the race to the center by the Republicans and Democrats as they presented themselves and their presidential nominees to the voters at the carefully choreographed 1996 national conventions.

In truth, the existing parties—one right of center and the other left of center—are well adapted to the American electorate. The extremes of the political right and left have few adherents in America. As a result, two centrist parties can accommodate quite well the vast majority of voters. As Key observed,

Certain patterns of popular political beliefs and attitudes mightily facilitate the existence of a dualism of parties. These patterns of political faith consist in part simply of the absence of groups irreconcilably attached to divisive or parochial beliefs that in other countries provide bases for multiparty systems. . . . Given . . . [the] tendency for most people to cluster fairly closely together in their attitudes, a dual division becomes possible on the issue of just how conservative or how liberal we are at the movement. Extremists exist, to be sure . . . but they never seem to be numerous enough or intransigent enough to form the bases for durable minor parties. (1964, 210)

Winning in the two-party context requires widespread support from diverse segments of society, and the desire to win leads to policy moderation and efforts to bring varied interests together. Americans want choices on election day, but they do not want losing to constitute a personal, group, or regional catastrophe (Polsby and Wildavsky 1996, 323). Thus far, the Republicans and Democrats may not have always fully satisfied the citizenry, but neither have their electoral victories created intolerable consequences for any significant element of society.

In fact, public opinion data demonstrate that Americans are more favorable to the existing party system than is commonly believed. It is true that polls have shown over 60 percent of the public favoring the formation of a new independent party. However, more revealing than voters' willingness to let more parties into the process are the indicators of public approval for the two major parties. A September 1995 poll, for example, found that only 12 percent felt that a new party should replace either one of the major parties (6 percent felt it should replace the GOP and a separate 6 percent thought it should replace the Democratic party). Further evidence that the public is not as disenchanted with the Republicans and Democrats as conventional wisdom would suggest comes from a 1996 Gallup poll conducted after the national conventions. This survey showed that 89 percent of respondents were favorable toward at least one major party, whereas only 11 percent were unfavorable, neutral, or unsure about both. Thus, if the core constituency for a third party is voters who are at least neutral about the two parties or downright negative toward them, then it would appear that only about one voter in ten met this criterion in 1996 (Moore 1996, 13).

For those asserting that there is a constituency for a new left of center party, the data are not encouraging. Among voters asked in 1994 how well each represented "people like yourself," 32 percent gave high marks to both parties, 21 percent did so for the GOP only, and 22 percent rated only the Democrats highly. Of the remaining 25 percent who were not satisfied with the Republican and Democratic parties, only 5 percent identified themselves as either liberal or very liberal (Moore 1996, 3).

Fostering Electoral Accountability

Democracy at its root is a system in which citizens have a relatively high degree of control over their governmental leaders (Greenstein 1970, 2). Admittedly, in the American constitutional system of separation of powers and federalism, officeholder accountability to the voters via elections is complicated and sometimes difficult to achieve. However, accountability is enhanced by having a relatively simple system in which there are only the Republicans and Democrats to hold accountable for the state of the Union.

Because elected officials want to keep their jobs and perpetuate their parties in office, they have a stake in coping with societal problems, or at least satisfactorily explaining their actions to voters. As election after election, especially presidential elections, has demonstrated, voters may not be highly informed on all the issues of the day, but they are perfectly capable of rendering retrospective judgments on the performance of a party in office—as the Democrats learned to their sorrow in 1994 and the Republicans did in 1992.

Elections do not provide elected officials with specific policy mandates. Candidates collect voters for different and sometimes conflicting reasons. In a system where there are many issues but only one vote for president or U.S. representative, it is not possible for elections normally to be mandates on specific issues. Rather, elections provide voters with an opportunity to render judgments on performance and a dualist party system makes this task infinitely more manageable for the voters than does a multiparty system.

Promoting More Effective Governance

Just as officeholder accountability to the voters within the American system of separation of powers and federalism would be vastly more difficult with a multiparty system, so too would effective governance. Policy making within our separated system requires extensive negotiation, bargaining, compromise, and cross-party alliances. Policy gridlock or at least delay is a constant threat even when the same party controls both the executive and legislative branches. It is hard to imagine how introducing a substantial number of third- or fourth-party representatives and senators into the mix would facilitate more timely or effective policy making. Organizing the House and Senate would become vastly more difficult and protracted, as would the negotiations required to produce legislation. In addition, splinter and extremist elements of society could well gain enhanced influence if their parties' support was required to organize a chamber or pass critical bills. Legislation essential to keep the government operating, such as budget resolutions, appropriations, and tax bills, not to mention crucial foreign policy measures, could well be held hostage by minor party legislators. How could a three- or four-party system with smaller and more cohesive parties than the existing congressional parties and with more polarized activists as their support base contribute much to the policy-making process other than delay, intensified conflicts, greater divisive-ness, and gridlock?

The potential for a governance breakdown would certainly not be lessened if a third- or fourth-party candidate were to emerge victorious in a presidential election (an unlikely event to be sure!) and then were required to deal with a Congress controlled by Democrats or Republi-cans. To say the least, the incentives for interbranch cooperation would not be great. Imagine for a moment, a President Ross Perot having to lead or negotiate with a Republican- or Democratic-controlled Con-gress. For people knowledgeable about national policy making and concerned about the well-being of the republic, it is not an inviting prospect.

It has been suggested that the two major parties are immobilized by having to promise too many things to too many people (Lowi 1996b, 47). Yet a clear-eyed review of recent history reveals that elec-tions really do matter and that policy changes can and do flow from shifts in party control of the presidency and from changes in the parti-san composition of Congress. The Great Society social programs of President Lyndon Johnson were possible only after the Democratic landslide of 1964; governmental retrenchment and the beginning of devolution of responsibilities to the states flowed from the 1980 elec-tion of Republican Ronald Reagan and the GOP gaining control of the Senate; and the end of Aid to Families with Dependent Children as a federal entitlement and its becoming a state responsibility—a major policy change—followed the Republicans winning control of Congress in 1994. The fragmentation of policy making and increased complexity of negotiations that would be occasioned by introducing third- and fourth-party legislators into the process would be more likely to create government inaction than to constitute a remedy for it.

Institutional Changes Required to Create a Multiparty System in the United States

As has been documented in this volume, a variety of institutional ar-rangements in the United States operate to encourage and perpetuate a two-party system and discourage multipartyism. A truly viable multi-party system would, therefore, require a change in some basic institu-tional arrangements to which, for the most part, Americans seem firmly committed. There is only the remotest chance that these institutions will be rearranged in the foreseeable future. Hence, much of the discus-sion about the United States developing a multiparty system is just that—a discussion of the hypothetical. Among the institutional arrangements that probably would have to be changed are the following widely accepted features of the political system: the direct primary system for nominating state and congressional officials, the presidential primary system, the single-member district-plurality system for electing the House, Senate, and state legislatures, and the separation of powers system. In addition, changes would be necessary to three less popular arrangements: the Electoral College, the Federal Election Campaign Act, and state ballot access laws.

An institutional arrangement that deserves special attention is the uniquely American system of nominating candidates through primary elections. This nominating process has helped to perpetuate a two-party system and contributed to the unprecedented Democratic–Republican electoral dominance for over 140 years. This Progressive era reform, which no realistic reformer is suggesting should or could be replaced by procedures that put party leaders in control of candidate selection, has had the effect of channeling dissent into the two major parties. In the United States, unlike other nations, dissidents and insurgents do not need to go through the difficult and often frustrating exercise of forming an alternative party. Instead, they can work within the existing two major parties by seeking to win major parties' primary nominations as a route to elective office, which is much more likely to yield success than the third-party or independent candidacy method. The primary nomination system makes American parties particularly porous and susceptible to external influences. In the process, the primary system reduces the incentives to create additional parties (Epstein 1986, 244–45).

Multiparty Politics at the State Level Has Been Overtaken by the Tides of National Politics

State politics in this century has seen several examples of multiparty systems in which third parties competed effectively with the major parties, notably in Wisconsin (Progressive party) and Minnesota (Farmer–Labor party). These were third parties that were at least temporarily successful despite the institutional arrangements that inhibit third parties. They won governorships, controlled state legislative chambers, and elected U.S. senators and representatives. The demise of these multiparty systems with their successful third parties is testimony to the difficulties third parties have operating within an electoral system in which voters align themselves in national politics between the two major parties, and then are required to align themselves among three parties in state elections. The Midwest's third parties died as separate entities in the 1940s and were forced to merge into the major parties because the tides of national politics became too strong within their respective states for them to survive. With partisan attachments being forged in the fires of national politics, it became impossible for parties like the Progressives of Wisconsin or the Farmer–Laborites of Minnesota to maintain their separate identities and retain a reasonable chance of electoral success. Leon Epstein has described the impact of national political alignments on Wisconsin's three-party system that operated in the 1930s and 1940s.

> When the Republicans were again effectively challenged after World War II, it was by the new state Democratic party whose leaders were very much in line with the northern liberalism of the national party, specifically with its presidential campaigns. The third-party Progressives had not been able to retain the loyalty of voters, who now, particularly in urban areas, identified with the Democratic party of FDR and Truman national politics. *The national electoral alignment was simply too strong a force to counter, and Wisconsin reemerged as an arena for competition between Republicans and Democrats.* (Emphasis added; 1986, 126)

More recently, state-level third parties formed around colorful prominent leaders, who once were statewide officeholders, have withered after these individuals ceased to head the ticket. Thus, former Republican U.S. Senator Lowell Weicker led his Connecticut party to victory in the 1990 gubernatorial election with 40 percent of the vote, only to see the party fade as an electoral force (19 percent of the vote) in 1994 when he was no longer a candidate. Similarly, the Alaska Independence party, with former Republican Governor Walter Hickel as its candidate, won the governorship in 1990 with 39 percent of the vote. However, without Hickel to lead the ticket in 1994, the party failed to retain the governorship and garnered only 13 percent of the vote for governor.

Although the tides of national politics have overwhelmed the midwestern states that once had viable third parties earlier in this century, recent research by James Gimpel suggests that some ingredients for multiparty systems do still exist in selected western states. These are states in which the partisan cleavages created by national and state politics are askew, thereby creating an opening for third parties. Gimpel concludes, however, that even in these western states there is virtually no prospect for development of electorally viable third parties because institutional arrangements (e.g., direct primary, single-member districts) that "push would-be third party voters to a choice of two candidates for office running under national party labels" are not apt to be changed in the foreseeable future (Gimpel 1996, 207).

Preserving the Two-Party System and Its Contributions to American Democracy

The historic role attributed to third and minor parties has been to raise and publicize issues of societal concern, and then force one or both of the majority parties to confront these problems, as exemplified by the Free Soil party (1848), People's party (Populists of 1892), Progressive parties of 1912 and 1924, American Independent party (1968), and the independent candidacy of Ross Perot in 1992. The fact that none of these parties achieved the presidency or majority status in a single chamber of the Congress is testimony to the ability of the major parties to adjust to these challenges and absorb many of the third-party dissidents into their own ranks. That the same two major parties have been able to so completely dominate electoral politics suggests that these institutions have the capacity and durability to adjust to the problems of the late twentieth and early twenty-first centuries as well.

There is even reason to believe that the much heralded role of third parties as the agents that publicize issues and force the major parties to adopt them may be exaggerated. For example, it has been claimed that the Socialist party platform advocating a minimum wage for twenty to thirty years was crucial to its gaining acceptance by the major parties. However, we have no way to know whether the minimum wage would have been adopted in the 1930s had there been no Socialist party. As Paul Allen Beck has noted,

> The evidence suggests . . . that the major parties grasp new programs and proposals in their "time of ripeness" when . . . such a course is therefore politically useful to the parties. In their earlier, maturing time, new issues need not depend upon major parties for their advocacy. Interest groups, the mass media, influential individuals, and factions within the major parties may perform the propagandizing role, often more effectively than a minor party. (1997, 49)

If the test of a viable party system is whether or not it has contributed to citizen control of their leaders, maintenance of political stability, and relatively effective policy making, then the American two-party system has met the test. Rather than concern themselves with giving greater play to third and minor parties, Americans would be better advised to pay attention to the problems being created for the two great major parties by the expanding influence within these parties of activists whose views are out of line with the preferences and concerns of party rank-and-file voters and the voting public in general.

Part II

Performance

5

Surviving Perot:
The Origins and Future of the Reform Party

John C. Green and William Binning

Much of the heightened interest in American minor parties results from two recent "figures": H. Ross Perot and his 19 percent of the presidential vote in 1992. Perot is a controversial public figure, an eloquent spokesman for "middle-class consciousness" but also an unpredictable and quixotic leader. And his 1992 vote figure was the second largest for a minor party this century, surpassed only by a middle-class revolt led by former President Theodore Roosevelt in 1912. Although Perot was much less popular in 1996, his 8.5 percent of the vote was still a solid showing. Indeed, put back to back, Perot's 1992 and 1996 campaigns garnered more support than any other minor party in American history.

What will be the legacy of this impressive performance? One can imagine two scenarios. First, the Perot effort may follow the path of other independent candidacies and decline, leaving behind new issues, activists, and voters to be absorbed by the major parties. Such a result would be hardly negligible since it could help reconfigure the major parties. Second, the Perot campaigns could develop into a viable minor party. Historically, such occurrences have been extremely rare, with only a few parties surviving their founders, let alone having any influence. Our task here is to assess these prospects. To put it bluntly, can the Reform party survive Ross Perot? We will conclude that while the first scenario is most likely, the special circumstances of 1992 and 1996 make the second scenario possible.

Viable Minor Parties

The scholarly consensus is that minor parties are an integral part of the American two-party system, serving as correctives to the failures of the major parties (Rosenstone et al. 1996). Since such failures vary in scope and type, so do minor parties. Although not mutually exclusive, the major parties can fail in at least three important ways (Guth and Green 1996). First, they can fail to offer plausible candidates, thus provoking campaigns by prominent personalities "independent" of their ranks. Such "personalistic" parties have been the most successful at the polls and hence are the best known. Second, the major parties can fail to address a critical issue, thus sparking protests that spill over into elections. These "protest" parties have been the most common kind of minor party in the United States. Finally, the major parties can fail to articulate a coherent ideology, thus encouraging the fuller expressions of political principles. Such "principled" parties have been the longest-lived type of minor party.

By this logic, minor parties could persist and prosper if they successfully institutionalized their response to major party failure. Such an eventuality could create a facsimile of a multiparty system in the American context. Such a *possibility* is a far cry from a *probability*, of course, and there are great obstacles to its realization. Theodore Lowi (1996b) makes the case for this possibility, and his argument is a useful guide for considering the Reform party's prospects.

Lowi suggests there are three minimal features for a viable minor party in the American party system. First, the party must be built from the bottom up, focusing on nominating and electing candidates at the state and local levels (Lowi 1996b, 51). After all, it is in these races that the major parties routinely fail to provide plausible candidates, thus offering opportunities for minor party activity. The chief obstacle to such a strategy is state election law, which routinely discriminates against minor parties. However, this obstacle can be overcome by dint of hard work and legal action. In this regard, the legalizing of fusion tickets is especially important.

Second, Lowi suggests that a viable minor party must not aspire to be a "governing" party but rather an "influence" party, dedicated to changing the political agenda (Downs 1957, 127–28). To that end, it must offer clear alternatives on issues the major parties fail to address—a common enough circumstance in a two-party system. By vigorously contesting elections on the basis of neglected issues, minor parties could serve as "honest brokers and policy managers" between the major parties (Lowi 1996b, 50). The chief obstacle here is the major parties themselves, who can readily mimic minor party issue positions. However, if minor parties carefully choose issues that convulse the major parties, this obstacle can be overcome. In this regard, gridlock or close divisions among the major parties present invaluable opportunities.

Third, Lowi argues that a viable minor party must develop a cadre of party activists dedicated to principles in politics—something the major parties regularly fail to articulate (Lowi 1996b, 50–52). Such an activist corps is the prime resource for minor parties, who cannot hope to attract the funds for the capital-intensive politics practiced by the major parties. Indeed, labor-intensive politics can be especially effective in subnational campaigns on neglected issues. The chief obstacle here is the nature of ideology: principles often breed inflexibility and factionalism. However, this obstacle can be overcome by the development of *partisanship*—that is, a simultaneous commitment to the minor party's principles and its organizational health. Thus a viable party needs dedicated partisans rather than zealous ideologues.

The first two of these features (bottom-up campaigns, issue focus) are strategic considerations that presume the third (dedicated partisans). Indeed, without a cadre of partisan activists, local, issue-oriented campaigns cannot be carried out with any effect. So the institutionalization of a viable minor party, whatever its origins, requires at minimum the development of a corps of partisans. In this regard, each type of minor party has strengths and weaknesses. The candidates at the head of personalistic minor parties can attract a large and loyal following, but such loyalty may not transfer into partisanship. The issues at the core of protest parties can also attract a large and enthusiastic backing, but such concerns may be too narrow to generate partisanship. The ideology at the center of principled parties can attract a host of energetic and committed activists, but such views may be too doctrinaire to produce partisanship.

Ross Perot and the Reform Party

How do these distinctions relate to Ross Perot? Overall, the Perot campaigns were good examples of a personalistic minor party, especially in 1992 (Ceaser and Busch 1993, 87–126). Simply put, there would have been no national campaigns or Reform party without Perot: in both 1992 and 1996 these efforts were extensions of his unique personality. Perot represented the epitome of candidate-centered politics that now dominates even the major parties. He was a well-known business leader and something of a celebrity before becoming a presidential candidate, and he used his notoriety, immense personal wealth, and media savvy to bypass normal political channels. Perot even replaced the usual tools of candidate-centered campaigns with techniques that focused on him: talk-show appearances, infomercials, electronic town meetings, and a cadre of grassroots volunteers tightly managed from Dallas by telephone, computer, and fax.

In many respects, the personalistic nature of Perot's 1992 campaign was the antithesis of the features Lowi identifies as necessary for a viable minor party: it was focused on the presidency rather than state or local races, its proclaimed goal was to govern rather than influence the government, and it did not give priority to developing a partisan activist corps. These limitations can be clearly seen in the way Perot chose to institutionalize the 1992 campaign. Instead of founding a party, he started an interest group, United We Stand America (UWSA), a "citizens lobby" dedicated to monitoring elected officials.

However, the 1992 Perot campaign left behind substantial resources for party building. It secured ballot access in most states, the possibility of federal public financing in future elections, a potent set of issues, and a large organization of volunteers. These resources are not inconsequential. It cost Perot approximately $14.5 million to get on the ballot in all fifty states, not to mention the massive volunteer effort. He spent another $54 million on the fall campaign, largely of his own money, which gave his effort credibility (Alexander and Corrado 1995, 132). It took a season of trial and error to develop his issues—including an embarrassing withdrawal and reentry into the campaign. And in 1993, UWSA had roughly one million members and $18 million in annual dues (Barnes 1993).

Although Perot received far fewer votes in 1996, his second campaign both exploited and enhanced these resources. Central to this process was the founding of the Reform party. In 1992, some of Perot's original activists wanted a new party, and despite Perot's own lack of interest, they founded the Independence party. This effort attracted an array of minor party activists, such as the left-leaning New Alliance party, which had run numerous candidates, including twice for president, in prior elections. The Independence party went through several transformations, finally becoming the Patriot party in 1994, and then developing sixteen state affiliates by 1995 (Lowi 1996b, 52; Bruni 1996; Salit 1996).

Meanwhile, considerable interest in independent candidacies and minor parties developed as the 1996 election approached. Numerous major party leaders considered independent presidential bids, including Jesse Jackson, Lowell Weicker, Bill Bradley, and Colin Powell. At the state level, there was a substantial increase in minor party activity as well, some of which enjoyed success at the polls. A good example was the New York Independence party's gubernatorial campaign in 1994, which qualified the party for the ballot access (Reform Party 1996a). Finally, many of Perot's followers were swept up in the Republican campaign in 1994 (Partin et al. 1996); both the successes and disappointments of the resulting GOP takeover of Congress intensified interest in a minor party.

Given these events, Perot came under increasing pressure to found a party, and he responded in typical Perot fashion. First, he organized a national convention of UWSA at Dallas in August 1995, where representatives of the major parties were invited to speak. Polls surrounding the event revealed that some three-quarters of UWSA members wanted to form a new party, and a good bit of organizing went on at the meeting itself. Then, on September 25, Perot announced the founding of the Reform party from the same forum where he announced his 1992 candidacy, the *Larry King Live* television program. He promised an all-out effort to establish a viable party, but declined to say whether he would seek its presidential nomination. As in 1992, this announcement launched a flurry of activity to get the Reform party on the ballot in all fifty states. As part of this effort, Perot reorganized UWSA in January 1996, essentially absorbing the group into the Reform party—and generating a lawsuit from disgruntled group leaders (Reform Party 1996b; Hall 1996a, 1996b).

By the summer of 1996, the Reform party was on the ballot in all states and the District of Columbia. Perot was listed under "Reform Party" in forty-three states, as "Independence" in New York, "Independent Reform" in South Dakota, and "independent" in Alabama, Delaware, Mississippi, Tennessee, Texas, and Wyoming (*Ballot Access News* 1996). These names reflect in part variations in state law, but also differences in how ballot access was achieved. In many states, Perot and UWSA activists went through an arduous petition or party registration drives. In other places, this chore was undertaken by state parties linked to Perot supporters, typically Patriot organizations. And in still others, such as New York, a ballot-qualified state party (the Independence party) allied itself with the Reform party. Overall, Perot spent $6.7 million to secure ballot access nationwide (Baker 1996a).

Perot next organized a national nominating convention for the new party in August 1996. Billed as an electronic town meeting, the convention took place in two places a week apart (Long Beach, California, and Valley Forge, Pennsylvania). These meetings were largely media events, dominated by speeches from Perot. The nominating of the party's presidential candidate was conducted by mail ballot. Because Perot had delayed announcing his intention to run for the nomination, he drew a reputable opponent: former Colorado Governor Richard Lamm, a Democrat, who teamed up with former California Congressman Edward Zchau, a Republican, as a running mate. Perot handily defeated the Lamm–Zchau ticket in the voting process, which was a logistical nightmare and widely believed to have been rigged in Perot's favor (*Associated Press* 1996). Perot further alienated some supporters by accepting $29 million in federal public financing (Corrado 1997). Accepting these funds limited Perot's contribution to $50,000 and necessitated an extensive private fund-raising effort that eventually netted some $11 million (Hall 1996c).

After the August convention, factionalism broke out within the new party, as various state leaders, many supporters of Lamm, tried to organize a "national committee" from the state Reform and allied parties. Perot eventually set up his own national committee at a meeting in Nashville, Tennessee, in January 1997. This meeting involved representatives from forty-two states and was characterized by bitter disputes between pro- and anti-Perot factions. In the end, Russell Verney, Perot's 1996 campaign manager, was chosen as national chair along with a cadre of Perot loyalists in other offices. The party promised a "real" national convention in October 1997 with delegates elected by Reform party members in all congressional districts across the country (Miller 1996).

Some of the anti-Perot factionalism came from individuals who ran on the Reform party ticket for state and congressional offices in 1996. All told, seven candidates for the U.S. Senate and thirty-six candidates for the U.S. House of Representatives and one hundred seventy-six state legislative candidates ran on the Reform or allied party tickets. Despite promises to help such candidates, Perot did very little on their behalf. Similarly, Perot had promised to endorse like-minded major party candidates, a fusionlike strategy followed by UWSA in 1994, but he did so just once, for William Weld in Massachusetts (Baker 1996b). Ironically, a bright spot in the fall election was the victory of five congressional candidates endorsed by the Reform party's New York affiliate, the Independence party; all were major party incumbents (two Republicans and three Democrats). The Independence party also endorsed 121 state legislative candidates in New York, most of whom were also Republican or Democrat. Of course, this result reflects fusion laws and local efforts rather than the national campaign.

Compared to 1992, the 1996 general election campaign was a desultory affair (Hall 1996d, 1996e). Polls consistently showed Perot with low single-digit support, and as a consequence, he was excluded from presidential debates and had trouble buying television time for his infomercials. He was unable to recruit a well-known running mate, finally settling on economist Pat Choate, hardly a household name. The campaign spent only some $27 million, about one-half the spending in 1992, and far less than expended by the major party nominees. Indeed, Perot was largely ignored until the very end of the campaign, when allegations of fund-raising irregularities by the Democratic National Committee and a weak performance by the Republican presidential ticket (including an eleventh-hour appeal for Perot to withdraw from the race) raised doubts about the major parties. On election day, Perot secured 8.5 percent of the vote, down from his 1992 showing in every state (see table 5.1). Maine was Perot's best state in both elections, reflecting its fabled political independence. He also did well in the West, followed by the Midwest and Northeast. With the exception of his home state of Texas in 1992, Perot was less successful in the South and in states with large minority populations.

All these episodes reveal both the limitations of Perot's personal appeal and the potential of the Reform party (Pomper 1997, 190–91; Nelson 1997, 62–66). Indeed, the fledgling party had numerous assets after 1996, including money in the bank (some $14 million on January 1, 1997), future public financing, ballot access, and a large following of voters and activists. Of these assets, the activist corps is by far the most important, and a good place to judge its future viability. The right-hand columns in table 5.1 provide a rough estimate of Reform party activist corps, based on the mail-in vote for the party's presidential nomination. While the raw numbers are encouraging, their magnitude in relation to the vote cast is not: the activist corps bears no direct relationship to the success of Perot at the polls in either election.

Reform Party Activists: The Case of Ohio

To what extent has the Reform party developed a strong activist corps? We can begin to answer this question with the results of a 1996 survey of Reform party activists in Ohio.[1] Ohio is a good place to observe these "Reformists" for several reasons. First, as one can see in table 5.1, Ohio ranked just above the middle of the states in terms of support for Perot in 1992 and 1996. Second, it also ranked among the top states in the absolute number of activists, but toward the low end of activists per voting population. Third, Ohio has seen a great deal of pro-Perot activity since 1992, all conducted by volunteers, and much of it spawning competing factions. And fourth, Ohio is a strong party state, where activists are likely to have had experience with traditional party organizations.

Partisanship

Are the Ohio Reformists strong partisans? Table 5.2 reports two common measures of partisanship and then a scale that combines both.

Table 5.1
Support for Ross Perot, 1992 and 1996

| | Votes | | Activists | |
	1992	1996	Number	Per voters*
Maine	14	13	79	0.42
Alaska	28	11	87	0.46
Idaho	27	13	353	0.73
Utah	27	10	147	0.23
Kansas	27	9	1052	1.00
Montana	26	14	226	0.56
Wyoming	26	12	458	2.21
Minnesota	24	12	677	0.32
Nebraska	24	11	182	0.27
Oregon	24	11	410	0.62
Washington	24	9	395	0.23
Nevada	24	93	24	0.73
Arizona	24	8	820	0.63
Vermont	23	12	47	0.19
North Dakota	23	12	213	0.81
Oklahoma	23	11	1758	1.46
Rhode Island	23	11	68	0.19
New Hampshire	23	10	264	0.53
Massachusetts	23	9	598	0.24
Colorado	23	7	1740	1.19
Missouri	22	10	555	0.26
Connecticut	22	10	409	0.30
South Dakota	22	10	101	0.31
Wisconsin	22	10	586	0.27
Texas	22	7	2582	0.46
Ohio	21	11	1425	0.32
California	21	7	17335	1.98
Indiana	20	10	1050	0.50
Delaware	20	10	156	0.91
Florida	20	9	3910	0.75
Michigan	19	9	1022	0.27
NATION	19	8	49266	0.54
Iowa	19	8	154	0.13
Pennsylvania	18	10	1060	0.24
Illinois	17	8	905	0.21
West Virginia	16	11	108	0.17
New Jersey	16	9	601	0.20
New York	16	8	1149	0.20
New Mexico	16	6	232	0.47
Kentucky	14	9	434	0.53
Hawaii	14	8	112	0.32
Maryland	14	7	560	0.33
North Carolina	14	7	746	0.30
Virginia	14	7	358	0.15
Georgia	13	6	767	0.33
Louisiana	12	7	79	0.04
South Carolina	12	6	822	0.73
Alabama	11	6	285	0.18
Arkansas	10	8	177	0.20
Tennessee	10	6	246	0.13
Mississippi	9	6	78	0.09
Washington, D.C.	4	2	54	0.31

*Number of Reform party activists divided by 1,000s of votes cast in 1996.
Source: Official Election Returns; *Ballot Access News* 12(7), September 1996.

Almost two-thirds of these activists considered themselves to be "members" of the Reform party. It is not clear what such membership means, however, as is demonstrated by the second measure of partisanship, the strength of attachment to the Reform party. Just under one-fifth of respondents claimed a "very strong" and just over one-quarter a "strong" attachment to the party. The remaining activists admitted to only "moderate" or "weak" connections.

In the second column of table 5.2, we combine these two items to produce a five-point scale comparable to standard measures of major party identification. The first category, "Core partisans," included both "members" and "very strongly" attached to the Reform party, and it accounted for just under one-fifth of the sample. The second category, "Solid partisans," included party "members" who were "strongly" attached, and it made up just under one-quarter. The next group of "Mixed partisans" lives up to its name: most were "members" with "moderate" attachments, but it also included "members" with weak attachments and nonmembers with "strong" or "very strong" attachments. This intermediate group made up just over one-quarter of the respondents. These first three categories are the equivalents of "strong," "weak," and "independent leaning" categories in standard measures of partisanship. The remaining two groups were called "Weak" (less than one-fifth of the sample) and "Peripheral" partisans (less than one-sixth); none claimed to be party "members" and each expressed "Moderate" and "Weak" attachments to the party, respectively.

So, only about one-fifth of Ohio Reformists were strongly committed to their party, a figure that is at least two or three times smaller than

Table 5.2
The Ohio Reform Party: Measures of Partisanship

Reform Party		Combined	
Member:	64.8%	Partisanship:	
		Core	19.3%
Attachment to		Solid	23.4
the Reform party:		Mixed	25.4
Very strong	19.8%	Weak	18.7
Strong	27.4	Peripheral	13.1
Moderate	37.5		
Weak	15.3		

Source: Survey by Authors, 1996.

comparable groups of major party activists (Green and Guth 1994). The remaining categories showed lesser degrees of commitment. While the Core partisans represented a good beginning for a new party, they probably could not sustain a viable organization. We can use these five categories of partisanship to explore more fully the attitudes of these activists.

How do these activists see the goals of the Reform party? We asked the respondents to chose among three: elect a good candidate (the principal goal of a personalistic minor party), protest poor policies (the key motivation of protest minor parties), or develop alternative principles in politics (the major reason for principled minor parties). As table 5.3 reveals, the Ohio Reformists overwhelmingly chose electing a good candidate, and this goal was the *most* popular among the Core and Solid partisans. Protest motivations increased as we moved toward the Peripheral partisans, while principled motivations were a minority position across the board.

This candidate-centered focus is further demonstrated in the second section of table 5.3, which reports on standard measures of incentives for politics. By far the most important motivation was "Back candidate," followed by other purposive incentives, such as "Promote issues" and "Civic duty." These motivations accounted for a majority of all five partisan categories, but declined from the Core to Peripheral partisans. In this regard, the Ohio Reformists resembled their major party counterparts, who were also strongly motivated by purposive incentives (Margolis and Green 1995).

Incentives that are more instrumental, such as "Win elections" and "Support party," were much less salient, however. Only among Core partisans did a majority report these things as "very important," and the percentages declined very sharply as we moved to the Peripheral partisans. There was even less interest in material and solidary incentives in all categories. It is here that the Ohio Reformists differed most from their major party counterparts (Margolis and Green 1995). Of course, these activists have had much less opportunity to contest elections, build their organization, and obtain personal rewards from politics.

How active are the Ohio Reformists? The last section of table 5.3 reports on three measures of party activity: the first two are self-assessments of involvement in the 1992 and 1996 campaigns, and the last is an index of career activism constructed from a battery of thirteen specific activities.[2] Almost two-thirds of the respondents reported being "active" or "very active" in the 1992 Perot campaign. As one might expect, activism was highest among the Core partisans and declined sharply to the Peripherals. Anticipated activism in 1996 showed a simi-

Table 5.3
The Ohio Reform Party: Motivations, Goals, Activity

	Core	Solid	Mixed	Weak	Peripheral	ALL
TOP PARTY GOAL:[1]						
Elect good candidates	66	63	63	51	55	58
Protest poor policies	19	17	27	36	36	26
Develop better principles	15	20	10	13	9	16
MOTIVATIONS:[2]						
Back candidate	93	86	86	75	77	84
Promote issues	83	82	71	66	65	74
Civic duty	76	67	68	52	55	64
Win elections	53	46	35	30	21	38
Support party	49	32	18	12	8	25
Business/employment	28	20	18	15	15	20
Fun/excitement	15	9	6	4	4	8
Social contacts	7	3	3	3	1	4
Political career	4	0	2	2	0	2
POLITICAL ACTIVITY:[3]						
Active in 1992	86	70	57	35	34	59
Active in 1996	85	66	32	22	9	46
Career activism	53	41	21	20	29	33

1. Columns add to 100%.
2. Entries are percent reporting each motivation to be "very important."
3. First two rows are percent reporting being "active" or "very active"; third row are percent who score in top two categories of activism index.
Source: Survey by Authors, 1996.

lar pattern, with comparable figures for the Core partisans, but a very sharp decline among the other groups, so that less than one-tenth of the Peripherals expected to be "active" or "very active" in the fall campaign.

Such self-reports probably overstate involvement, of course, and must be viewed with some skepticism. Nevertheless, these patterns match the index of career activism: the Core partisans claimed to have been most active prior to the Perot campaigns and the other groups much less so. (The Peripheral partisans were a modest exception to the pattern because of previous participation in local GOP politics.) These data reveal three things. First, most Reform party activists were aroused by the initial Perot campaign, but there was a significant influx of new people in 1996. Second, the strongest Reformists exhibited a spillover of past participation, a pattern found in national samples of Perot activists (Partin et al. 1996). And finally, with the exception of the Core partisans, the Reformists were far less active than their major party counterparts in Ohio (Margolis and Green 1995).

We also asked these activists about their previous partisan attachments and if they still identified with the major parties. The Ohio Reformists came from diverse partisan backgrounds: almost two-fifths had been Republicans, one-third independents, one-quarter Democrats, but just 1 percent were members of other minor parties. Interestingly, the former Democrats and minor partisans were concentrated among the Core partisans, former independents peaked with the Mixed partisans, and former Republicans were most common among the Peripherals. Present-day major party identification fits this pattern. Almost two-thirds of Core and Solid partisans identified as independents, and about one-quarter leaned Democratic. About one-half of the Mixed partisans were independents, with the rest leaning evenly toward both major parties. The Weak and Peripheral partisans contained large pluralities of Republicans (data not shown).

Overall, then, we can conclude that the Ohio Reform party activists are not particularly strong partisans. Only a small group had the psychological attachments, motivations, and activity levels comparable to major party activists in Ohio. And even the Core partisans were largely motivated by the personal appeal of Perot rather than protest issues or ideological principles.

Leaders, Issues, and Ideology

This last point is amply illustrated in table 5.4, which reports the activists' "net proximity" to political leaders and organizations.[3] As one might expect, Perot himself was quite popular. However, note the pattern of support: the overwhelming backing in the first three categories declined to a net of zero for the Peripherals. Thus, the strongest Reformists were the most committed to Perot personally.

These activists showed less support for other prominent figures. Ralph Nader was quite popular with the Core partisans, largely on the basis of his reputation as an antiestablishment figure, but Nader's support declined in the other categories and was negative among the Peripherals. A weaker and opposite pattern occurred for Colin Powell: the Core partisans were divided while the Peripherals were modestly supportive. Note that Richard Lamm, Perot's challenger for the Reform party nomination, was not well liked anywhere and was strongly opposed by the periphery of the party. Bo Gritz, the Populist party candi-

Table 5.4
The Ohio Reform Party: Proximity to Leaders and Groups

% Net Proximity[1]	Core	Solid	Mixed	Weak	Peripheral	ALL
Ross Perot	+87	+89	+80	+55	0	+70
Ralph Nader	+54	+15	+32	+ 4	-17	+20
Colin Powell	+ 2	+19	+10	+21	+27	+14
Richard Lamm	-6	-23	-28	-34	-54	-27
Bo Gritz	-16	-39	-34	-45	-74	-39
Bill Clinton	-59	-60	-39	-46	-37	-49
Bob Dole	-66	-39	-45	-16	-10	-38
United We Stand	+97	+96	+87	+59	+22	+77
Chamber of Commerce	- 8	+ 8	+ 1	- 7	+10	+ 1
Sierra Club	+ 7	- 1	+ 9	-10	-20	- 1
NRA	- 2	- 1	-23	- 7	-28	-11
AFL-CIO	- 1	-10	-14	-25	-53	-15
Christian Coalition	-21	-16	-35	-33	-40	-28
ACLU	-55	-54	-37	-52	-52	-49

1. Entries are percent net proximity to leader or group; positive sign indicates closeness and negative sign indicates distance.
Source: Survey by Authors, 1996.

date in 1992, was no better liked than the "progressive" Lamm. Not surprisingly, the major party nominees were uniformly disliked, particularly toward the core of the party.

These patterns extend to prominent political organizations as well. Perot's "citizens' lobby," United We Stand America, was very popular among the strongest partisans (most of whom were members) but, as with Perot himself, much less so at the periphery. A host of other interest groups garnered only modest backing from any of the categories. The Chamber of Commerce and the Sierra Club were the least unpopular, but the NRA, AFL-CIO, Christian Coalition, and ACLU were all disliked with varying degrees of intensity. These data confirm previous findings on Perot activists: they were both "pulled" by attraction to Perot and "pushed" by repulsion from major party candidates and interest groups (Partin et al. 1996). These push–pull factors were clearly the strongest for the Core partisans.

What about the political opinions of the Ohio Reformists? Table 5.5 reports on issue positions and ideology. Note first that all five categories strongly backed staples of Perot's critique of the political sys-

Table 5.5
The Ohio Reform Party: Issues and Ideology

% Net Agree[1]	Core	Solid	Mixed	Weak	Peripheral	ALL
Pro campaign reform	95	87	87	80	63	84
Pro term limits	84	84	84	72	66	80
Pro balance budget	79	87	72	70	43	72
Pro reorganization	62	62	53	49	64	58
Anti NAFTA/GATT	85	61	52	46	20	55
Anti immigration	77	60	65	52	40	51
Pro national health	38	37	45	17	13	33
Pro regulation	37	35	46	29	32	37
Pro abortion	35	24	28	35	37	30
Anti affirmative action	33	51	42	54	38	44
IDEOLOGY[2]						
Very conservative	22	19	18	22	39	23
Conservative	23	34	24	32	21	28
Moderate	40	40	47	32	28	38
Liberal	8	4	5	13	6	7
Very liberal	7	3	6	1	6	4
THE SYSTEM NEEDS[2]						
Fundamental reform	70	52	48	45	45	52
Major changes	12	23	25	33	31	24
Better leaders	18	25	27	23	24	24

1. Entries are net agreement with issue position.
2. Columns add to 100%.
Source: Survey by Authors, 1996.

tem, such as campaign reform and term limits. As with support for Perot himself, support fell somewhat as we move from the core to the periphery. A similar pattern obtained for issues central to Perot's critique of the federal government, such as the need for a balanced budget and the reorganization of federal programs.

However, a big surprise occurred on elements of Perot's economic nationalism, such as opposition to NAFTA and GATT and restrictions on immigration. Here the Core partisans were quite enthusiastic, but support dropped off very quickly, so that the Peripheral partisans were for free trade and immigration. Finally, there were mixed patterns on other economic issues (national health insurance and business regulation) and social issues (abortion and affirmative action). These patterns confirmed previous evidence on the opinions of Perot's supporters: they were simultaneously antigovernment and antiestablishment (Greenberg 1995, 234–37).

Although the Ohio Reformists were not consistent ideologues in a conventional sense, they did think of themselves as right-of-center. Even among the Core partisans, only one-sixth identified as liberals. The number of conservatives rose fairly steadily from two-fifths at the core to three-fifths at the periphery, while the number of moderates fell from two-fifths to less than one-third. However, there was some modest evidence that an "ideology of reform" was developing among the Core partisans. We asked the respondents to choose from three remedies for the American political system: fundamental reform, major changes, or the recruitment of better leaders. On balance, the sample chose fundamental reform, and the Core partisans did so by the largest margin. When combined with standard questions on "purist" political style and trust in political institutions, these data suggest that the closer one gets to the Core partisans, the stronger the commitment to procedural reform. And by the same token, the closer one gets to the Peripheral partisans, the less consistent the interest in such matters.

Despite their differences, the Ohio Reformists shared a deep sense of betrayal by the political system. They fit well descriptions commonly applied to Perot supporters in 1992: a "radicalized middle-class" that is "estranged from the power centers of society" and motivated by a "compelling and simple idea: elites are corrupt" (Greenberg 1995, 231). This pattern was certainly evident in the demography of the Ohio Reformists. White, male, middle-aged, and solidly middle class, they reported being disconnected from the social institutions that structure mainstream society, from churches and civic associations to interest groups and political parties (Greenberg 1995, 237–41). In this regard, the Core partisans differed in modest, yet significant ways from the Peripherals: the former are younger, with greater family responsibilities and fewer economic prospects. These circumstances are particularly conducive to the development of a "middle-class consciousness," of which an "ideology of reform" could be a central feature, and Reform partisanship the final product.

Surviving Perot

What can we conclude from this review of the Reform party? Clearly the most likely scenario is that Ross Perot and his followers will fade into the history books, following the well-worn path of independent candidates. The limits of Perot's personal appeal, his dominance of UWSA and the Reform party, and the limited development of a corps of partisan activists all suggest that the Reform party will not prosper. Indeed, violations of Lowi's three minimal prerequisites for a minor party make it likely that it will not survive Ross Perot. This does not mean that Perot will leave no political legacy: the issues, activists, and voters aroused by his presidential campaigns may help reconfigure the major parties.

It is possible, however, for the Reform party to defy the odds, survive its founder, and alter the party system itself. The peculiar circumstances of the 1992 and 1996 campaigns left the party with numerous assets, from funds to ballot access, not the least of which was the rudiments of a partisan activist corps. Although not yet well developed, the Core partisans we observed in Ohio could grow in size and scope. If they can transfer their loyalty for Perot to their party, they have the opportunity to broaden their appeal to the Peripheral partisans and beyond. And they also have the chance to develop an "ideology of reform" that might tap "middle-class consciousness" to challenge the major parties on a regular basis.

Notes

1. In the summer and spring of 1996, a mail survey was conducted of all the circulators of Reform party petitions in Ohio in the fall of 1995. The response rate was excellent: a single wave produced a return rate of 50 percent, excluding undelivered mail (N = 497). There was no apparent bias in the returned survey by geography or gender. Since this sample had been quite active in circulating petitions, it contains fewer peripheral participants than other surveys of Perot activists (cf. Partin et al. 1996).

2. The thirteen activities include primary voting, signing petitions, contacting public officials, attending campaign rallies, attending public meetings, writing letters to the editor, door-to-door canvassing, making a campaign contribution, participating in a demonstration, serving as a party official, recruiting volunteers, running for public office, and raising funds. The index summed any positive response to these questions over the lifetime of the respondent.

3. Here "very far" and "far" responses were subtracted from "close" and "very close" responses. A positive sign indicated net closeness and a negative sign indicated the opposite.

6

Taking the Abnormal Route: Backgrounds, Beliefs, and Political Activities of Minor Party Candidates

Christian Collet

One of the more interesting developments in party politics over the past few years has been the emergence of independent and minor party candidates and the challenge they have posed to the major parties in American elections. Today, there is greater public acceptance of and interest in alternative parties than at any time in recent history, and a number of national and state figures have run for office as independents or formed their own party organizations (Collet 1996). New parties, such as Natural Law, are emerging with slates of candidates, while older ones, like the Libertarians, are institutionalizing. Whether it be Ross Perot, Harry Browne, or Ralph Nader at the presidential level, or Angus King of Maine, Walter Hickel of Alaska, or Lowell Weicker of Connecticut at the state level, minor party candidates have risen to prominence across the board. If it is true, as Ambrose Bierce once wrote, that "to be independent is to be abnormal," then the abnormal route to political office is becoming increasingly popular.

Despite growing public interest and attention, minor party candidates remain somewhat of a puzzle. What kinds of people run for office on a minor party ticket? What prompts them to leave conventional politics and choose the "abnormal" route to office? What has been their political experience? What do they hope to accomplish for themselves and for their party? These are important questions not only for what they say about the candidates and their parties, but also for what they suggest about the broader party system. Minor party candidates are the most prominent symbols of discontent with the major parties, but they are also, as Walter Dean Burnham (1970) has put it, "forerunners" of political change: raising new issues, representing new groups, and offering new ideas for public policy. Examining the beliefs, backgrounds, and political activities of minor party candidates can thus provide important insights into the American political process.

This chapter undertakes just such an examination. Unlike previous studies that have focused exclusively on the presidential level, my concern will be with minor party candidates who have run in subpresidential elections. I begin by looking at trends in minor party candidacies in recent elections. I then shift from aggregate to individual-level data and take a closer look at the candidates themselves with a survey of minor party candidates conducted after the 1994 elections. In the conclusion, I discuss the implications for the findings and the uniqueness of contemporary minor party movements.

The Rise of Minor Party Candidates in Subpresidential Elections

Many observers and the media have begun to recognize the growth and appeal of minor party and independent candidates at the national level. But few are aware of what may be a more important trend in lower level elections. Figure 6.1 shows the number of minor party and independent candidates running in gubernatorial and congressional elections in the thirty-year period between 1964 and 1994.[1] With the exception of the mid-1980s, the growth in candidates has been steady since the 1960s. It reached an apex in the 1992–94 cycles, when a combined 910 minor party candidates were on federal and statewide tickets—over 3.5 times as many as in the 1964–66 cycle. When one also considers the nearly 2,800 minor party candidates that ran for the state legislature over the same two-year period between 1992 and 1994, roughly twice as many as in 1968, one is apt to agree with David Gillespie's claim that "this is the most fertile period since the Great Depression for third parties and independent movements" (quoted in Balz 1994).

Along with the growth in candidacies, there has also been a growth in the number of minor parties. But unlike the gradual trend witnessed in Figure 6.1, the increase in parties has been sudden and explosive, as shown in Figure 6.2. From the mid-1960s to 1970, the number of minor parties in gubernatorial and congressional races gradually increased, more than doubling from fourteen to thirty-four. But in the twenty-year period through 1990, the number of parties stabilized in the mid-thirties. In 1992, however, the total erupted to sixty-nine, more than four times as many as in 1968, and more than twice as many as in 1980. In 1994, the number of parties declined somewhat to fifty-one, still substantially higher than at any other time in the past quarter-century. Although some of the increase in parties may be attributable to individuals mounting independent candidacies and giving themselves a party label, the number of genuine minor parties has clearly grown. In

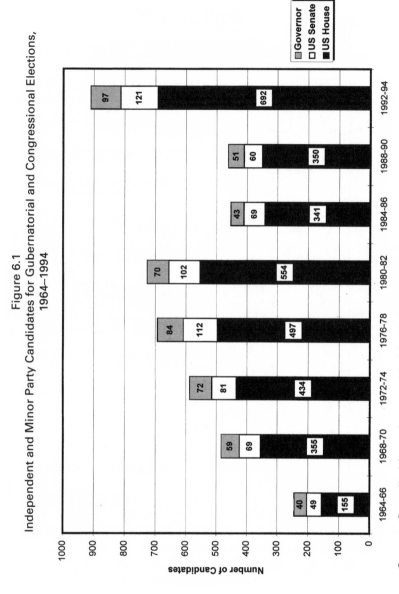

Figure 6.1
Independent and Minor Party Candidates for Gubernatorial and Congressional Elections, 1964–1994

Source: Compiled from data provided by *America Votes.*

Christian Collet

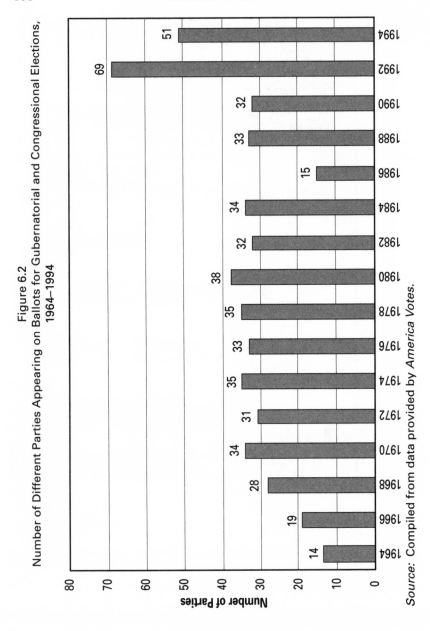

Figure 6.2
Number of Different Parties Appearing on Ballots for Gubernatorial and Congressional Elections, 1964–1994

Source: Compiled from data provided by *America Votes.*

California, for example, three new parties qualified for the ballot in the span of four years.

Expectations about Minor Party Candidates

Throughout American history, the rise and decline of minor parties has been associated with the performance of the two-party system. When major parties satisfy their constituencies, individuals channel their political energies through them; when they fail, individuals are often led or pushed in other directions, looking for ideological, partisan, or issue satisfaction. As Austin Ranney and Willmoore Kendall explain,

> the number and strength of minor parties in American politics at any given time is a measure of how much extreme discontent exists. And that, in turn, is a measure of how well or how badly the major parties . . . are performing their task of giving each major group in the community enough satisfaction to keep it moving in the mainstream. (1956, 458)

Simply put, eras of vigorous minor party activity occur when major party performance is at a nadir.

Thus discontent with the major parties lies at the foundation of any minor party or independent candidacy. But what, specifically, might account for a candidate's decision to abandon the major parties and run against them? Some might suggest economic reasons, such as the state of the national economy. When the economy is doing poorly, class politics becomes more salient, and people turn against the parties in power. The economy or another crisis might produce a "new powerful issue" that divides the major parties. Agrarian discontent and slavery led to major party breakdown, minor party emergence, and eventual realignment in the middle and late nineteenth century (Sundquist 1983). In more recent times, civil rights and the Vietnam War have been cited as polarizing issues that inspired alternative party activity (Mazmanian 1974; Hazlett 1992).

In contemporary times, however, a minor party candidacy may be predicated more on an individual following or personal ambition. The weakening of major party organizations, along with technological developments, have made it easier in the twentieth century for "independent-minded candidates" to "take the plunge" (Rosenstone et al. 1996, 121). This can have two implications. First, minor party candidates might be led away from the major parties by a charismatic leader, such as George Wallace or Ross Perot. Second, minor party candidates might run to satisfy their *own* ambitions to campaign for public office. This may occur because the major parties have denied access to such candidates or simply because the alternative route is preferred.

Minor party candidates tend to vary demographically, depending on the ideological leanings of their party. "New politics" parties, like some left- and right-wing parties, draw the younger and less affluent (Kitschelt 1990; Müller-Rommel 1989; Elden and Schweitzer 1971; Canfield 1984); centrist parties, such as the Perot movement, are somewhat older and more affluent (Partin et al. 1994). But, across ideological spectrums, alternative party activists have been found to share two common social denominators found among political elites, namely a high level of education and male gender. Also, they are often "composed of the heterodox of major parties," meaning that they have had some experience with the two parties and have chosen to reject them (Duverger 1963, 291). Although some candidates may have been mobilized into political action by their current party, many likely defected from the ranks of the Republicans and Democrats (Mazmanian 1974).

What are their qualifications and political experience? Because of the limited potential of minor parties to achieve power, along with the stigma that accompanies the abandonment of conventional politics in American two-party culture, well-qualified politicians have traditionally eschewed minor parties (Rosenstone et al. 1996, 38). As a consequence, candidates that do run under minor party banners are usually less well known, and have less governing experience—what David Canon (1990, 1993) has referred to as "hopeless" or "experience-seeking" amateurs. Financial and resource limitations make their campaigns difficult and the limited attention they receive from the press discourages an active campaign.

Given the long odds, why do they bother? What motivates them? Standard theories of rational action postulate that most candidates strategically contemplate the electoral environment, and weigh the costs, benefits, and the probability of winning before mounting a campaign for office (Black 1972; Rohde 1979; Jacobson and Kernell 1983; Canon 1990). But since there are many costs and few benefits for minor party candidates, it seems likely that they would have other motives: to help the party organization; to protest and provide an alternative; to express views on issues or ideology; to satisfy personal reasons, ambition, and even the "thrill of the battle." Some might even run out of a sense of "citizen duty"—a feeling that it is the proper responsibility of a citizen to actively participate in politics (Maisel 1982; Huckshorn and Spencer 1971; Canon 1990).

Because of the conditions for their formation and their small size, minor parties are thought to be ideologically cohesive, fervently partisan, and highly committed. Whether making a dramatic "bolt" from the major parties, or simply pursuing an independent ideological course, minor party activists are expected to rally around their issues or leaders and work energetically to promote them. Candidates, of course, are no different. As the most public representatives for their party, they would presumably be even more partisan and committed than the party's rank-and-file activists.

Let us summarize our expectations about minor party candidates. First, one would expect these candidates to be overwhelmingly male and well educated, with some diversity in age and income. Second, we expect "the heterodox of major parties" to reflect a previous affiliation with either the Republicans or the Democrats. Given the costs of abandoning conventional politics in America, some candidates may have been involved with *both* major parties before exploring minor party activity. Third, many would point to a "defining moment" for why they left the major parties: a specific issue, event, or individual leader. And some may point to ideological concerns, personal ambition, or for lack of a specific reason, general dissatisfaction with the major parties. Fourth, most minor party candidates probably have little experience and are less active campaigners, and so campaign out of a sense of party commitment, ideological zeal, or citizen duty. Finally, one would expect the partisanship of minor party candidates to be fervent and strong, with singularity of purpose and ideological purity.

Data and Methods

The data used to test these expectations come from a survey mailed to every minor party candidate who ran for governor, the U.S. Senate, the U.S. House, or a state legislature in thirty-six states in the 1994 elections.[2] The survey was distributed in two waves: the first to the western states in January 1995, and the second to the remaining states in May. Of the 1,082 surveys delivered, 584 completed replies (with 34 undeliverables) were received, resulting in a response rate of 55.7 percent. In total, the original sample included representatives of forty-five different parties.

Because of its cross-sectional nature, the sample naturally favored the parties that were the most active and fielded the most candidates in the 1994 elections. As a consequence, there were nearly twice as many Libertarian respondents (58 percent) as respondents from other parties. The varying sample sizes among the parties were accounted for by controlling the data by party group. The parties were sorted into five categories: "old" left, "new politics" left, centrist, "new politics" right, and "old" right (see appendix).[3] This categorization is based on two factors: the candidates' self-reported ideological position of their party on a seven-point scale, and bibliographic information provided by the parties or secondary sources.

Social and Political Backgrounds

Like most candidates for state or congressional office, minor party candidates display some of the characteristics of social elites (Herrnson 1995; Putnam 1976). As table 6.1 shows, they tend, overall, to be older, well-educated, and male. They are also racially homogeneous, with only "old" left parties having more than one-quarter nonwhites. However, with the exception of centrist, Libertarian, and new right candidates, most are middle class. Some of these elite traits differ across the party categories. As expected, the members of the new politics parties are younger, reflecting the recent generations who are attracted to such movements. Generally, left party candidates have more education, but paradoxically less income.

Most candidates were previously affiliated with one, or both, of the major parties (table 6.2). Fewer than one-quarter (24 percent) had no prior contact with Republicans or Democrats, whether as a lifelong member of a minor party or as a newcomer to their current party. Overall, it was the new politics parties that brought the most people into alternative politics: 19 percent of new left candidates and 23 percent of new right candidates had no prior party affiliations. By contrast, the centrist and old right candidates came largely from the two-party system (77 percent and 73 percent, respectively).

For the most part, right party candidates defected from the Republican Party, while left party candidates defected from the Democrats. Centrist candidates were almost equally mixed between the major parties. Noteworthy percentages of new politics candidates—especially Libertarians—came from the opposite party, however, reflecting their party's ability to transcend the current ideological spectrum. The table also reflects some partisan ambivalence; roughly one in seven candidates reported that they had been *both* Republicans and Democrats.

Only in rare instances did a single issue, event or individual leader compel a candidate to abandon the major parties (table 6.3). Examples are right party candidates motivated by abortion and centrist party candidates attracted by a state or local leader such as Lowell Weicker. Few pointed to economic factors, and even fewer to personal ambitions. Instead, the most popular explanations—even among newer parties—

Table 6.1
Social Characteristics of Minor Party Candidates

	Total	Old Left	New Left	Centrist	New Right	Old Right
Age						
18-24	2%	3%	3%	4%	2%	1%
25-34	16	10	10	15	20	7
35-44	3	26	42	22	37	21
45-54	28	21	35	19	25	37
55-64	13	23	8	22	10	18
65+	9	18	2	19	6	15
Race						
White	87%	70%	85%	77%	88%	94%
Black	2	5	0	8	2	1
Latino	1	13	2	4	<1	0
Asian	1	3	2	0	1	1
Other	9	10	12	12	9	4
Education						
H.S. or less	23%	19%	13%	4%	25%	27%
2-year college	15	10	13	24	15	16
B.A./B.S.	36	36	45	28	37	29
M.A./Ph.D.	26	36	28	44	23	28
Income						
<$20,000	15%	11%	22%	12%	14%	14%
$20,000-39,999	31	34	34	31	28	37
$40,000-59,999	23	29	19	19	23	21
$60,000-79,999	13	13	7	12	14	12
$80,000+	19	13	19	27	20	16
Sex						
Male	80%	57%	69%	80%	88%	76%
Female	20	43	31	20	12	24
(N)	(561)	(38)	(57)	(26)	(336)	(104)

Note: Some columns may not total 100 percent due to rounding.

Table 6.2
Previous Party Affiliation of Minor Party Candidates

	Total	Old Left	New Left	Centrist	New Right	*Old Right*
Republican	37% (208)	5% (2)	11% (6)	35% (9)	40% (133)	56% (58)
Democratic	26 (145)	58 (22)	53 (30)	42 (11)	19 (64)	17 (18)
Both	14 (78)	13 (5)	14 (8)	8 (2)	15 (50)	13 (13)
Another minor party	5 (25)	11 (4)	4 (2)	8 (2)	3 (11)	6 (6)
No previous party affiliation	19 (105)	13 (5)	19 (11)	8 (2)	23 (78)	9 (9)
(N)	(561)	(38)	(57)	(26)	(336)	(104)

Note: Columns may not total 100 percent due to rounding.

were rooted in ideology and a general sense of major party failure. Many Libertarians, for example, claimed they feared that their former party (usually the Republicans) was becoming too much of a contributor to the growth of government. Several candidates across the board claimed that there was no difference between the major parties, while many candidates in the old left claimed that their previous party (mostly the Democrats) had moved too far to the right.

Responses concerning general party failure were the most common. Many on the left pointed to their former party's ineffectiveness and inability to address issues of importance to them. Similarly, left candidates complained that their previous party no longer represented them or their social group. Centrists and right candidates pointed instead to major party hypocrisy, inconsistency, and abandonment of traditional principles. Some even grumbled ambiguously about major party "corruption." Right, left, and center party candidates alike mentioned that they felt that their previous party was elitist, although old left candidates voiced this complaint most often.

Table 6.3
Reasons for Leaving Major Parties by Minor Party Candidates

	Total	Old Left	New Left	Centrist	New Right	Old Right
Defining moment						
Specific Issue(s)	6%	0%	2%	5%	3%	18%
Supported Individual	0	0	0	5	0	0
Specific Event	2	10	2	0	1	0
Economic reasons						
Personal/Pocketbook	1%	0%	0%	5%	1%	0%
National/Sociotropic	3	0	0	5	3	3
Ideological Reasons						
Party became too statist	16%	0%	0%	0%	23%	11%
Party moved too far left/right	4	10	2	5	3	4
No difference between two parties	8	7	12	5	7	8
General Party Failure						
Party was ineffective	9%	7%	20%	14%	8%	7%
Party unrepresented	7	20	10	9	5	4
Party abandoned principles	8	3	5	14	7	12
Party broke its promises	8	3	5	5	10	6
Party was corrupt	2	0	2	5	1	2
Disliked party leaders	5	7	2	5	5	3
Party was elitist	5	13	7	5	4	6
Personal Reasons						
Preferred minor party	10%	7%	20%	9%	10%	3%
Wanted to promote career	1	3	0	0	0	1
Country needs alternatives	1	0	0	5	1	0
Had no say in politics	2	4	0	0	2	2
Miscellaneous	8%	7%	10%	5%	7%	9%
(N)	(444)	(30)	(42)	(23)	(259)	(90)

Note: Column totals may slightly exceed 100 percent due to rounding and a few economic reasons falling under the heading of specific issues (e.g. taxes, budget deficit) being counted in both categories. N in parentheses.

Political Experience, Campaign Activity, and Motivations

Minor party candidates have little experience running for office, are not active campaigners, and give partisan, ideological, and civic duty explanations for mounting their campaigns (table 6.4). But within these patterns, there are striking differences between the new politics and others parties' candidates. Candidates involved in the new politics parties are not only newcomers to their parties, but also to politics as well. Meanwhile, the old right and old left candidates have more experience. Centrist party candidates are mixed, having been around politics for longer periods of time, but having only recently become involved with their parties. This pattern surely reflects the relative youth of some of these party organizations, many having been formed in the past five years.

Some candidates have garnered political experience within their parties, with nearly half having held a position in their party's leadership. The job titles ranged from national chair to county committee member or secretary. Candidates from the old left and old right parties were more likely to have been in their party's leadership, indicating that such parties indeed offer more experienced candidates, but they may have a harder time than new politics parties attracting individuals outside the leadership to run for office.

The number of times the candidates had previously run for office also reflects the new–old party divide. Candidates in the older parties are more seasoned, with well over half from both the old left and old right having run for office more than once. Centrist party candidates also reflected more campaign experience, but probably under a previous party banner. Contrasting the old politics parties and the centrists are the candidates from the new politics parties—especially the new left, ecological parties—most of whom were running for the first time in 1994. But for many of these candidates, this experience may be just the beginning: nearly two-thirds of new politics candidates, and three-fifths of the entire sample, said they would be willing to run for office again.

What kinds of campaigns do minor party candidates wage? The candidates were asked to identify the electioneering techniques they employed in the 1994 campaign, from a list of thirteen popular activities (walking precincts, engaging in debates, posting signs, phone solicitation, hiring consultants, hiring pollsters, using direct mail, appearing on television or cable TV, appearing on radio, producing videos, making speeches, holding fund-raising events and dinners, and traveling through their districts). Based on the total number of responses, candidates were placed into one of four categories: "barely

Table 6.4

Political Background, Experience and Activity of Minor Party Candidates

	Total	(N)	Old Left	New Left	Centrist	New Right	Old Right
Active in Politics							
0-2 years	24%	(137)	12%	35%	15%	27%	14%
3-10 years	42	(243)	29	42	41	47	32
11-24 years	22	(127)	29	13	22	18	35
25+ years	13	(73)	31	10	22	8	19
Involved with Party							
0-2 years	22	(125)	10	35	52	16	33
3-10 years	49	(278)	35	63	36	56	27
11-19 years	18	(99)	20	2	4	22	13
20+ years	12	(65)	35	0	8	6	26
Leadership in Party	46	(262)	53	53	46	41	57
Ran for Office							
Once	47	(270)	39	66	33	48	39
2 times	25	(142)	15	22	26	28	19
3+ times	29	(166)	46	12	41	24	42
	63	(352)	64	64	56	65	61
1994 Campaign Actvity [1]							
Barely active	27	(159)	21	12	7	35	19
Somewhat active	23	(135)	29	24	30	23	21
Active	36	(210)	36	39	44	35	38
Very active	13	(76)	14	25	19	7	22
Reason for Running							
Party duty	22	(117)	22	31	5	27	7
Ambition	11	(57)	5	10	9	11	12
Issues	13	(69)	16	15	23	8	24
Citizen duty	18	(96)	32	25	5	15	21
Ideological	32	(170)	24	19	50	35	30
Spite/to oppose someone or something	4	(22)	0	0	9	4	7

Note: Columns may not equal 100 percent due to rounding.

1. Activity levels based on item asking respondents to identify how many of thirteen activities they pursued in their election campaign (e.g., posting signs, appearing on radio, engaging in debates). "Barely active" candidates were those who identified 0–2 items; "somewhat active" candidates identified 3–4 items; "active" candidates identified 5–7 items; "very active" candidates identified 8 or more items.

active" (if they identified 0–2 items), "somewhat active" (3–4 items), "active" (5–7 items), and "very active" (8 or more items). By this measure, only 13 percent of the candidates overall were in the "very active" category, and another 36 percent were "active," leaving roughly one-half of the sample as "somewhat" or "barely" active campaigners. New left, centrist, and old right candidates were among the most active.

Minor party candidates run for office for a variety of reasons: to help their party, to articulate their ideology, or simply to answer the call of citizen duty. Ideology surfaced as the most popular motivation overall—especially by candidates from the center to the right. As one Libertarian explained, "I ran for office because I wish to exterminate as much government as possible." The citizen duty response was more popular from left-leaning candidates. "I feel people should do some part in government instead of complaining. It's not enough to vote," said another candidate. New politics candidates expressed the most desire to help their parties, while centrists and old right candidates expressed the least, reporting instead greater concern with issues and ideology. Overall, only about one in ten candidates admitted to running for personal reasons, such as ego gratification or political ambition. Explained one candidate: "I wanted to learn the process so when I do it for real, I'll know how." Another was more succinct: "I run because I want to get elected, of course." The fewest responses, though, came in the category of spite, or running because of anger or opposition to another candidate. Typical of these responses was a comment from a Green candidate, who claimed to have run because "the incumbent in my district is terrible, and he would have been unopposed if I hadn't run."

Partisanship of Candidates

The partisanship of candidates can be determined by asking how the candidates voted, how committed they are to their party, or how much their party should compromise with other parties. Surprisingly, these candidates were weak partisans, regardless of the measure used (Table 6.5). For example, just over half reported voting for their own party's presidential candidate. In this regard, the new politics parties were among the strongest partisans, with 77 percent of the Libertarians and 58 percent of the ecological new left parties supporting their own presidential candidate. While many old left and old right stated that they always supported their party's entire ticket, little more than half reported voting for their own party's presidential nominee. Centrist candidates, being largely tied to local or state organizations, usually had

Table 6.5
Partisanship and Loyalty of Minor Party Candidates (cells report
percentage strongly agreeing or agreeing with the statements)

	Total	(N)	Old Left	New Left	Centrist	New Right	Old Right
1. % that report voting for their own party's presidential candidate in the 1992 election[1]	56%	(184)	24%	58%	0%	77%	10%
2. I would vote for the Republicans and Democrats if they stood for more of my party's positions.	53	(305)	43	60	59	48	64
3. I always support all of the candidates on my party's ticket.	52	(302)	61	61	15	54	46
4. Our party should consider forming a coalition with one or more minor parties so we can improve our chances at success.[1]	29	(99)	44	41	35	22	40
5. I am committed more to helping my party win than to advancing my own political philosophy.	26	(149)	15	40	26	25	23
6. It is better to be a firm party supporter than a political independent. [2]	22	(125)	42	15	11	23	17
7. My party should be willing to compromise so that it can attract more supporters.	12	(67)	14	0	26	15	2

1. Question asked of second wave of respondents only.
2. Item derived from 1980 National Election Study.

no presidential candidate to support, but more than half said that they always backed their party's own ticket candidates.

The candidates' weak partisanship is evident in their responses on other measures of partisanship (table 6.6). More than half said they would support the major parties if they were to adopt more of their own party's positions, and only one in four said that they were "committed more to helping [their] party win than to advancing [their] own political philosophy." On this latter measure, the new left candidates stand out, with 40 percent answering affirmatively. But when asked if it is better to be a firm party supporter than a political independent, only 22 percent agreed. Even candidates from the most partisan new politics parties valued independence over partisanship.

Openness to compromise can also measure the strength of partisan feelings and loyalty. No party had more than one-half of its candidates agree with the statement "our party should consider forming a coalition with one or more minor parties so we can have a better chance at success." Candidates from left parties were generally more supportive of building coalitions, perhaps reflecting recent efforts by Greens, the New Alliance party, and other progressive parties to coalesce their movements (Affigne 1995). But left parties, like all the other candidates, opposed the idea of their party using compromise as a strategy to attract more supporters. Only a little more than one in ten agreed, with the weakest support coming from new left and old right candidates.

The Prospects for Minor Party Candidates

In sum, minor party candidates are similar to their major party counterparts in some ways and different in others. Like most political elites, they tend to be white, male, and well educated. But of course they are also defectors, having abandoned one (and occasionally both) of the major parties. This defection usually occurred for ideological reasons or out of a general sense that the major parties were failing. So far, their experience as candidates remains fairly limited. Only one-half ran what were deemed to be "active" campaigns. Most seem to be ideologically driven, and in most cases, commitment to ideology seemed to exceed commitment to their party.

When one combines the independence, inexperience, and ideological motivations of minor party candidates with the enormous structural disadvantages facing minor parties in the United States, one cannot be overly sanguine about the prospects for substantial electoral gains. It is important to recall that despite their recent growth and visibility, and some isolated successes, most minor party candidates have not done any better, on average, at the polls. The mean vote percentage for gubernatorial and U.S. House candidates was merely 3 percent in 1992, when Ross Perot collected 19 percent. In U.S. Senate races the same year, it barely exceeded 2 percent. Indeed, minor party voting in congressional races was higher in the 1960s (and considerably higher in the 1890s) than it is today.

Some of this pattern may be a function of the political environment. Contemporary minor parties are more diverse than in previous eras. In prior waves of vigorous minor party activity (e.g., the 1890s) candidates emerged in turbulent times in dissent over divisive national or regional issues (Sundquist 1983). Such movements were often class-based, faced easier ballot access requirements, and had more "complete" party organizations operating on a national or regional scope (Winger 1995; Rosenstone et al. 1996; Key 1964). Minor party candidates were thus more concentrated geographically, more unified under similar party labels, and linked to the national movement and its presidential candidate. In the present era, candidates are more entrepreneurial, campaigns are more media-driven, and politics is more pluralistic. Thus minor party movements have become more diffuse. Rather than being mobilized by one crisis, or a set of related problems as they were in the past, minor parties and candidates are forming and running today for a variety of reasons, often out of a broad ideological discontent or a vague sense of major party failure.

This situation may be both an advantage and a disadvantage to minor party candidates. On the up side, candidates and parties are less linked to specific issues that can quickly be co-opted by the major parties. As a consequence, minor parties may be more likely to endure than in the past. On the down side, it is harder for them to develop electoral support. If minor parties and candidates base their existence on abstract protest or a doctrinaire outlook, their appeal to the voting population will remain marginal. Moreover, with a variety of active minor parties in America today the competition becomes greater for protest votes cast against the major parties. While a single third party movement in prior eras was able to tap into enough discontent to make substantial electoral gains, the myriad movements active today make it difficult for any opposition party to marshal enough support to win.

Although the old left and old right parties remain protest-oriented, and centrist parties remain candidate-centered, the new politics parties offer some interesting possibilities. Rather than sprouting up on the fringes of the major parties in response to a divisive issue, they are neither left *nor* right, but rather positioned around the "postmaterial" political dimension (Müller-Rommel 1990). As Ronald Inglehart

(1990) posits, younger generations have undergone a "culture shift" that has led to a change in values from basic economic needs ("materialist") to more "quality of life" and "self-expressive" issues (such as civil liberties and the environment). These interests and the parties forming around them, such as the Libertarian, Green, and Natural Law parties,[4] do not fall on the classic, left–right materialist dimension of politics, but rather on a new political dimension bisecting left and right (Inglehart 1987; Flanagan 1987). Being deeply rooted in ideology rather than in fleeting issues, new politics parties will likely persist for some time—especially if future generations continue to be drawn to them. Although they are younger and less experienced, the candidates from these parties revealed the weakest attachments to the major parties and reflected the strongest sense of commitment to their own. While the Green party has had notorious internal difficulties because of its members' philosophical opposition to hierarchy, the Libertarian and Natural Law parties have demonstrated an ability to develop and organize that should help them in the long run.[5]

Although their success remains scattered and their futures questionable, minor parties and candidates have, nonetheless, made a difference. Overall, the increasing numbers of parties and candidates have made elections more crowded and more interesting. The term "third-party candidate" has become more awkward, as it has become common in many state races to see fourth- and even fifth-party candidates. In an era of closer competition between the major parties, this situation has also meant a greater opportunity for minor parties to "spoil" elections, or at least deny the winner a majority share of the vote. In 1994, there were ten gubernatorial and U.S. Senate races where the winner received less than 50 percent, and three races where the winner got less than 40 percent. In the House, twenty-two victorious major party candidates received less than half the votes cast in their districts. Thus, while minor parties are often *individually* impotent, they can occasionally wreak *collective* havoc on the major parties.[6]

Most important, though, is that minor parties and candidates are becoming more active *despite* the many institutional barriers that continue to face them. While many candidates are still too inexperienced and doctrinaire to be thought of as serious contenders, they promote new issues and protest errant policies offered by the establishment. Even if today's candidates are not tomorrow's officeholders, they are laying the foundation for organizational growth. Although it may still be considered somewhat "abnormal" to be an independent or minor party candidate in the United States, it is becoming less so. The true measure of success for minor parties and candidates will be to see just how "normal" they become.

Notes

1. The data in figure 6.1 are grouped into four-year periods so as to eliminate the natural fluctuations in gubernatorial candidacies that occur between on- and off-year elections. Although the number of seats up in Congress are consistent every two years, the number of gubernatorial races varies.

2. States include: Alaska, Arizona, California, Colorado, Connecticut, Delaware, District of Columbia, Florida, Hawaii, Idaho, Illinois, Indiana, Iowa, Kansas, Kentucky, Maine, Massachusetts, Michigan, Minnesota, Mississippi, Missouri, Montana, Nevada, New Hampshire, New Jersey, New Mexico, New York, Oregon, Pennsylvania, Rhode Island, South Dakota, Texas, Utah, Vermont, Washington, Wyoming. The state of Alabama had no minor party candidates running. Candidate address lists were never received for Georgia, Louisiana, Tennessee, West Virginia, and Virginia. A few surveys in the first wave of mailings were sent to candidates in major local races in Hawaii (6), California (1) and Montana (1). In states where cross-endorsements were permitted (e.g., New York), questionnaires were distributed only to those candidates who ran on a minor party ticket *without* a major party endorsement. Because the survey contained questions that dealt with many party-related issues, such as major party departure and alternative party loyalty, candidates who were listed on their state's ballot as "unaffiliated" or "independent" were excluded.

3. There may be some ambiguity over the terms "old" and "new" to describe these party groups, since these labels have been applied to very different movements in the United States and abroad. The greatest confusion may come from the term "new right," a term often synonymous with "religious right." In comparative politics, "new right" has referred to authoritarian movements (Flanagan 1987). But here "new right" refers to Libertarians, since they represent the "new politics" branch that has grown from American conservatism. In the work on alternative social movements in Western Europe, there has been a tendency to lump Libertarian and Ecology parties into the same categories (e.g., Herbert Kitschelt's [1990] "left-libertarian" parties), but there was no justification for doing so in this case. American Greens clearly grew out of the "left"—and see themselves as very liberal—but Libertarians, in large part, can draw their roots to the laissez-faire economic theories that are fundamental to the American right. Furthermore, most Libertarians have some ties, past or present, to the Republican party, and, when willing to classify themselves ideologically, say they are "conservative." The Libertarians and Greens do have some similarities as "new politics" parties, but because of their very different social bases, and their occasional differences on the role of government, they were placed in separate categories.

4. The Natural Law party was founded in 1992. It qualified in 32 states for that election, and, according to their literature, fielded 175 candidates from president to state office. In the 1996 elections, they ran 177 candidates for U.S. Congress alone.

5. By the end of 1994, the Libertarian party reported having 132 elected members across the nation, ranging from school board to state representative (Personal communication, National Libertarian Party). The Green party had an unofficial count of 12 elected members, their highest being on the county board of supervisors in Hawaii (Personal communication, Green Party of California). In addition, members of the Peace and Freedom party in California and the Alaska Independence party have also won at the local level.

6. In the 1994 election for governor in Alaska, three small party candidates took a combined 19 percent of the vote in a race that was decided by 0.3 percent between Democrat Tony Knowles (who won) and Republican Jim Campbell. The 1994 race for governor in Connecticut was similar: three small party candidates combined for 31

percent of the vote in a contest decided by 3.5 percent. The gubernatorial race between George Pataki and Mario Cuomo in New York saw small party candidates take a combined 6 percent in a race that Pataki won by 3.4 percent. Pennsylvania's gubernatorial campaign featured three small party candidates who got a combined 15 percent of the vote in a campaign that was won by Republican Tom Ridge by less than 6 percent. In 1992, the U.S. Senate contest in California between Bruce Herschensohn and Barbara Boxer featured three small party candidates who took over 9 percent of the vote combined. Boxer won by less than five points. In New Hampshire, four candidates took a total of 6.5 percent in a race that Republican Judd Gregg won by less than three points. There are still other examples. Al D'Amato's reelection to the Senate from New York by 1.2 percent may have been impacted by the presence of five small party candidates who earned a total of 3.3 percent of the vote. In Hawaii, Frank Fasi, the longtime mayor of Honolulu and a favorite of native Hawaiians, formed his own Best party in 1994 and finished second in a four-candidate race for governor with 30.7 percent. He edged out Republican Pat Saiki by 1.5 percent.

Appendix[1]
Categorization of Minor Parties

Party Type	Score[2]	Party	States	N
Old Left	1.0	DC Statehood	Washington, D.C.	1
	1.0	Gun Control	WA	1
	1.0	Liberty Union	VT	3
	1.0	Progressive	VT	2
	1.0	Tax the Rich	CT	1
	1.0	Democracy in Action	NJ	1
	1.5	Peace and Freedom	CA, AK	21
	2.0	Socialist	OR	1
	2.0	New Alliance	IN	1
	3.8	Liberal	NY	7
	NR	Socialist Workers	UT, WA	2
	NR	Worker's World	MI	1
			Total =	42
New Left	1.5	Grassroots	IA, MN, VT	5
	2.0	Green	AK, CA, HI, ME, MN, NM, NY	26
	3.8	Natural Law	CO, CT, IA, NJ, VT, WA	30
			Total =	61
Centrist	3.8	Independent Fusion	NY	7
	4.0	A Connecticut Party	CT	2
	4.0	Good Neighbor	PA	1
	4.0	The Right Choice	RI	1
	4.0	Independent	MN	1
	4.0	Taxpayers Against Excess	PA	1
	4.0	Concerns of the People	CO	1
	4.4	Best	HI	5
	4.5	Alaska Independent	AK	3
	4.7	Independent	ME	4
			Total =	26

continued on next page

continued from previous page

Party Type	Score[2]	Party	States	N
Old Right	5.0	Cool Moose	RI	1
	5.5	Independent	CT	4
	5.8	American	OR, UT	9
	5.8	Conservative	NY	13
	6.0	United Independent	IL	1
	6.0	Patriot	WA, PA	5
	6.0	Constitutional	PA	1
	6.2	Right to Life	NY	29
	6.2	Independent	UT	5
	6.2	Independent American	NV, UT	20
	6.3	Concerned Citizens	CT	3
	6.9	American Independent	CA, AK	10
	7.0	Keep America First	NJ	1
	7.0	Taxpayers	KY, CO, WI	7
	7.0	LaRouche	NJ	1
				Total = 110

1. Four parties were not classified, and hence dropped, because of a lack of available information about their ideology and issue positions: People of Vermont (Vermont), Fed Up party (New York), Federalist party (Minnesota), Capitalist party (New Jersey). Two parties, Worker's World and Socialist Workers, were classified as "old left" based on knowledge of their ideology only, since their respondents gave no response (NR) to the item on party placement. Because it is based only on our sample of candidates, we do not intend this table to be an exhaustive list of minor parties or of the states where they are active.

2. Mean Party Placement Score (1-7).

7

Multiparty Politics in New York

Robert J. Spitzer

New York Republican party leaders knew that they faced an uphill battle in their effort in 1994 to unseat popular three-term Democratic Governor Mario Cuomo. New York had not elected a Republican governor since 1970, and statewide voter enrollment favored the Democrats by a wide margin. To buttress the chances of their candidate, George Pataki, Republican leaders quelled the gubernatorial challenge of the state's Conservative party by offering a spot on the state ticket to a Conservative party activist (the Conservative party was not satisfied with Pataki's conservative credentials). This helped ensure that Pataki would win endorsement by that party. In addition, the Republicans created a new party line expressly to help Pataki's campaign. With his name appearing three times on New York ballots, Pataki won a narrow upset victory over Cuomo. His margin of victory was 173,798 votes. Most of those who voted for Pataki did so on the Republican line, although Cuomo received more votes on the Democratic line than Pataki did on the Republican line, but Pataki also received 328,000 votes on the Conservative line, and 54,000 votes on the additional party line set up by the Republicans. Did the extra endorsements make a difference? Party leaders thought so. As one state Republican party leader noted, the added lines offered "a perception that [the extra lines] give non-Republican voters an alternative" (Fisher 1994).

New York State poses a fascinating and instructive example of a uniquely American hybrid of a two-party system that retains major party dominance while ensuring a stable and enduring minor party role. The New York case offers a feasible archetype for a vigorous electoral system. It also underscores the decisive importance of electoral/legal structures in shaping party politics—in particular, its rules for party recognition and the cross-endorsement rule.

History and Political Culture

The development of New York's minor parties can be traced both to the state's political culture and to state law. Both factors intertwine and converge to produce New York's distinctive electoral map. Yet the history that gave rise to the state's multiparty political culture could not have occurred without the accommodating web of laws.

New York has witnessed the emergence of no fewer than fourteen recognized minor parties during the twentieth century.[1] Of these, three have maintained an automatic slot for all elections on the state ballot since the late 1970s. These three, in order of formation, are the Liberal party, the Conservative party, and the Right-to-Life party. Two newer parties, the Independence and Freedom parties, joined the list after the 1994 elections.

The oldest of these, the Liberal party, was an offshoot of the American Labor party (ALP). The ALP was formed in 1936 by a group of socialists and trade unionists seeking a way to support President Franklin Roosevelt and other liberal-leftist candidates without working through the corrupt state Democratic party, then dominated by Tammany Hall (Karen 1975). The success of the Labor party in bargaining with the major parties was such that it attracted more radical elements, and in 1943 many of the original founders, including labor leader Alex Rose, broke away and formed the Liberal party. The ALP lapsed from existence in 1954, but the power of the Liberal party grew. Dominated by Rose until his death in 1976, the Liberal party has generally sided with liberal Democratic candidates, although it has occasionally supported moderate Republicans. Over the years, it has sought to promote such causes as full employment, consumer rights, rent control, progressive taxation, equal rights, and expanded social welfare programs (Moscow 1948; Zimmerman 1981). The party's primary power base has traditionally rested with urban Jewish voters, located mostly in New York City. In the 1980s and 1990s, however, it has sought to expand its base by trying to win black and Hispanic support.

The Conservative party was also founded as a result of dissatisfaction with a major party. After his election as governor in 1958, Nelson Rockefeller dominated New York's Republican party until 1974, when he resigned to become vice president. But Rockefeller's brand of liberal Republicanism was distasteful to many traditional conservative Republicans, especially in the business and professional class, and a group of them combined in 1961 to offer a conservative alternative to Rockefeller Republicanism. They also hoped to pressure the Republicans to move to the right (Schoenberger 1968). The Conservatives have generally identified with conservative Republicans, especially after

Rockefeller's departure, although they too periodically support conservative Democrats. In some more conservative upstate areas, the Conservative nod is pursued with equal vigor by Democrats and Republicans (Hannagan 1989). In the 1980s, the conservative perspective received a boost because of the election of Ronald Reagan as president. This national ideological swing has helped the party maintain its position as the state's third largest party.

The Right-to-Life party (RTLP) entered New York's political fray in the 1970s. But whereas the Conservatives and Liberals were founded by political activists and business leaders, the RTLP began inauspiciously among a book discussion group in the home of a Merrick, Long Island, housewife. The party's grassroots beginning was prompted by attempts in the state legislature to liberalize the state's abortion law. Those attempts succeeded in 1970, and the concerns of these formerly apolitical individuals with antiabortion sentiments accelerated when the Supreme Court ruled in *Roe v. Wade* (1973) that women had a right to a safe, legal abortion (Spitzer 1984). Unlike New York's other minor parties, the RTLP is predicated on a single issue—opposition to abortion. The salience of this issue for some New York voters was evidenced when, in 1978, the RTLP succeeded in establishing its own line on the New York ballot after a brief attempt to work within the major parties (notably, party founder Ellen McCormack sought the Democratic party nomination in 1976). Aside from fielding candidates in state races, the RTLP has also run minor party candidates for president. Unlike the state's other minor parties, however, the RTLP has operated under several handicaps. First, as a single-issue party that is generally considered extremist and inflexible, it often drives away many candidates (including many who consider themselves strongly antiabortion) who would otherwise jump at a chance to obtain an extra ballot line. Second, New York State is one of the most strongly pro-choice states in the nation; thus RTLP endorsement is often considered a net liability, especially for a candidate who already has a major party endorsement (Spitzer 1987, chs. 2 and 3).[2] This verdict is reflected in the RTLP's sometimes precarious fortunes. In the 1982 gubernatorial election, its candidate received just over 52,000 votes, dropping the RTLP ballot position to fifth from 1983 to 1986. This election dip caused RTLP leaders to seek a more well-known gubernatorial candidate for 1986. They turned first to the Republican–Conservative nominee, Westchester County Executive Andrew O'Rourke. But despite his own opposition to abortion, O'Rourke declined the endorsement based on the belief that an RTLP endorsement would actually cost him more votes than it would gain (Lynn 1986). The RTLP turned next to a Democrat, Nassau County District Attorney Denis Dillon, who initially declined the offer because "they approached me on the basis of saving the party." Although initially unwilling to jeopardize his political career for the RTLP, he finally accepted so that he could "talk about the lives being killed by abortion" (Neumeister 1986).[3] Dillon waged a vigorous campaign, and received 130,802 votes. In 1990, the RTLP turned to a Staten Island consultant and Republican, Louis Wein, who received about 137,000 votes. In the 1994 gubernatorial race, RTLP candidate Robert Walsh garnered 67,750 votes—just enough to maintain the party's status through 1998. Over the past decade, the party has fielded fewer candidates than ever for congressional and state legislative contests.

The two newest state parties were founded in 1994. During that year's gubernatorial election, millionaire businessman Thomas Golisano ran for governor on what was initially called the Independence Fusion party. Emulating the campaign approach at the presidential level of Ross Perot, Golisano spent his own money on an extensive media advertising campaign, and gained over 217,000 votes in the general election—enough for his party, renamed the Independence party after the election, to win the fourth spot on New York ballots (below the Democrats, Republicans, and Conservatives). Based in Rochester, the Independence party has endorsed many candidates, including Republicans and Democrats as well as independents, for local and state office. In 1995 alone, it endorsed about a thousand candidates. In 1996, Ross Perot used this line for his presidential bid. According to the party's state chair, its primary goal is to link up with other, similar third parties in other states (including the Perot movement) in order to create a coherent national third party. Its issue concerns include ballot initiative and referendum options, stemming the influence of political action committees, and other government reform proposals (*Syracuse Post-Standard* 1995; Kriss 1995).

The other party emerging from the 1994 elections was the Freedom party. While other state minor parties have found alliance with a major party, the Freedom party went beyond this in that it was expressly created by state Republican party leaders to boost the candidacy of gubernatorial candidate George Pataki. For what was initially called the Tax Cut Now party, Pataki received 54,000 votes on this line, qualifying it as an established party. The Freedom party is run out of Albany by state party leaders, and is available only to Republican candidates (Kriss 1995). As a direct creature of the state Republican party, it represents the clearest expression yet of the value attached to multiple endorsements.

New York's Electoral Structure

To understand how electoral structures encourage parties in New York, one must begin with the initial establishment of a party. According to state election law, a political party may establish an automatic ballot line for all New York elections by fielding a candidate for governor who receives at least 50,000 votes on that party line in the general election.[4] If this threshold is reached, the party is guaranteed a ballot position in all New York elections for the next four years (until the next gubernatorial election). If no automatic ballot slot exists for a party or candidate, an individual seeking statewide office must obtain at least 20,000 petition signatures (signature requirements are less for non-statewide offices). Any registered voter may sign an independent candidate's petition, regardless of the voter's party affiliation, unless the voter has already signed a competing candidate's petition.

In comparison with ballot access requirements in other states, New York's is one of the more demanding.[5] Despite this fact, however, determined and organized third parties can endure in New York where they cannot in other states by virtue of another characteristic of state law—the cross-endorsement rule. This key provision of New York election law says simply that parties may nominate candidates already endorsed by other parties. The votes that candidates receive on all of their lines are then added together in the final count to determine the winner. This practice traces to the post–Civil War era, when political opponents of New York City's powerful Tammany Hall political machine would join together in what were called "fusion" movements. Fusion candidacies incorporated multiple endorsements, but were usually associated with "good government" groups opposed to political machines. Such fusion efforts were common in the United States in the nineteenth century, but they declined by the end of the century when most states banned multiple party endorsements.[6]

Today, nine other states permit candidates to be endorsed by more than one party: Arkansas, Connecticut, Delaware, Idaho, Mississippi, South Carolina, South Dakota, Utah, and Vermont (Greenhouse 1996).[7] But the ability to cross-endorse does not alone explain New York's vigorous third-party activity, as New York's previously discussed distinctive political culture is also a vital factor. Third parties face tough going in Connecticut, for example, because state law there sets a 20 percent gubernatorial vote threshold as a requirement for party recognition. Even so, former Connecticut Senator and Governor Lowell Weicker succeeded in organizing and establishing a new minor party in the state, called A Connecticut party, in 1990, riding that party to the governor's office. In 1992, the party cross-endorsed incumbent Democratic Senator Christopher Dodd in his successful reelection bid (Yarrow 1992).

Cross-endorsement is a regular feature in New York elections. Not surprisingly, the Conservative party usually sides with the Republicans, and the Liberal party with the Democrats. Since 1974, for example, every Democratic candidate for governor has also been endorsed by the Liberal party, and every Republican gubernatorial candidate has won the endorsement of the Conservative party, except for the 1990 Republican gubernatorial nominee, Pierre Rinfret (he will be discussed later).

The cross-endorsement system has a number of consequences for the New York party system, the sum total of which cause New York to resemble, in certain respects, European multiparty systems. First, this provision removes a major impediment to voters casting votes for minor parties—that is, the "wasted vote" syndrome. Voters frequently have preferences for third-party candidates, but refrain from voting for them because of the feeling that they are throwing away their vote on a candidate or party that cannot win. But according to the cross-endorsement rule, votes cast for a candidate anywhere on the ballot are added to the candidate's total.

Second, one can easily calculate how many votes a party contributes to a candidate by observing the vote count on each line. Many quickly point out that a candidate would probably receive about the same total number of votes whether he or she appeared on one line or several. It surely seems likely, for example, that George Pataki would have defeated Mario Cuomo in 1994 whether his name appeared only once or three times on the ballot. Nevertheless, candidates perceive that every line helps, and it is all but impossible to dismiss the prospect that some electoral outcomes might be altered with the inclusion of one or more extra ballot endorsements.

Beyond this general supposition, some voters do feel more comfortable supporting a candidate with an alternative party label. In New York City's 1989 and 1993 mayoral elections, for example, Republican Rudolph Giuliani actively sought the Liberal party nomination because of the belief that many Liberal and Democratic voters in the city would be more likely to support him on that line than on the Republican line (Roberts 1989). Evidence of the importance candidates attach to multiple party endorsements can be seen in the frequency of cross-endorsements. To take the 1996 elections as a typical example, of New York's thirty-one representatives in the House, twenty-six were elected with more than one party endorsement, and the winners averaged just over two endorsements per House member. Of New York's sixty-one state senators, fifty-two were elected with more than one endorsement, and they averaged about 2.5 endorsements per senator. Of New York's 150 state assembly races, 120 won election with more than one endorsement, and they averaged over 2.3 endorsements. The great concern for cross-endorsement is all the more notable given the fact that the incumbent reelection rate for members of Congress is over 90 percent; for state legislative races, incumbent reelection in recent years has ranged from 97 to 99 percent. Despite the belief that these endorsements are crucial, a study of all New York state senate races from 1950 to 1988 demonstrated that third-party endorsements provided a winning edge for candidates in only about 3 percent of the races (Shan 1991, 45).

Third, minor parties may go beyond merely offering an additional line by offering the only line for a candidate denied a major party line. While not a common occurrence, there have been instances of major party candidates denied a major line who have gone on to win election on a minor party line. In 1969, then incumbent Republican New York Mayor John Lindsay was defeated in the Republican primary by John Marchi. But Lindsay was nevertheless reelected by running on the Liberal party line, defeating Marchi and conservative Democrat Mario Procaccino. It was later said that, as a reward for Liberal party support, no Liberal party activist seeking a municipal job went without work. In 1970, the Conservative party succeeded in electing one of its own, James Buckley, to the U.S. Senate in a three-way race against the Democratic nominee, Richard Ottinger, and the liberal anti-Nixon Republican incumbent, Charles Goodell.

Fourth, minor parties can run their own candidates, or endorse others, to punish major party candidates by depriving them of votes. In 1966, the Liberal party ran the popular Franklin D. Roosevelt Jr. for governor, instead of endorsing the Democratic candidate, Frank O'Connor. Incumbent Nelson Rockefeller was considered vulnerable to defeat that year, and the over half-million votes garnered by Roosevelt deprived O'Connor of the election (he lost by 392,000 votes). Alex Rose, then the leader of the Liberal party, commented later that the move to nominate someone other than the Democratic nominee was sparked at least partly by a desire for retribution against Democratic leaders who were so sure of victory with or without Liberal support that they brushed aside attempts by Rose to have influence in the process of nominating the Democratic candidate (Karen 1975). Indeed, influence over major party nomination decisions is often a key objective of minor party leaders.

Finally, minor parties can nominate candidates before the major parties try to influence the choices of the major parties. Recent New

York politics is replete with examples. In 1980, for example, an unknown town supervisor from Hempstead, Long Island, Alfonse D'Amato, received a critical early boost in his campaign for the U.S. Senate by winning the nomination of the Conservative party (he was later endorsed by the RTLP as well). Using that endorsement as a political jumping-off point, he then went on to challenge and defeat four-term incumbent Jacob Javits in the Republican primary. To complicate matters, however, Javits remained on the ballot because he had already earned the nomination of the Liberal party. Meanwhile, the Democratic nominee and reputed front-runner, Elizabeth Holtzman, found her otherwise open path to the Senate blocked by Javits's presence on the ballot. In the election, the state's liberal and moderate votes were split between Holtzman and Javits. Javits polled over 10 percent of the vote; D'Amato won by about 1 percent over Holtzman.

Anxiety over this "tail wags dog" syndrome in the 1980s encouraged leaders of both major parties to propose that the cross-endorsement provision be wiped from the books. A Democratic party resolution, considered briefly by state party leaders, denounced cross-endorsements: "The process has led to many cases where the people able to dispense such cross-endorsements obtain influence out of all proportion to the people they represent" (Carroll 1982a).[8] Similar sentiments have been expressed by the Republicans (Lynn 1982; Carroll 1982b). Despite this uneasiness with third-party influence, the major parties have lived with insurgent parties and factions for many decades, in part because these insurgent party movements served to vent public displeasure arising from disclosures of corrupt and autocratic major party practices in the first half of the twentieth century. Those minor parties that survived, such as the Liberal party, soon made their peace with the major parties. If major party bosses had succeeded in suppressing dissident reformist parties, enhanced public outrage might have cost the bosses control of their own party machines. This possibility caused party leaders to at least tolerate the existence of these dissident elements. As the case of the new Freedom party demonstrates, major state parties have now discovered a new means for using and controlling the multiparty options to their direct benefit.

These five factors outline a significant degree of electoral potency for New York's minor parties, and it is evident that the major parties are often uncomfortable with the extent of minor party influence. Successful moves to change the system have been blocked in recent years, however, by a state legislature populated with representatives who have benefited from the system.

Minor Party Leverage

New York's third parties are interested in maximizing their influence, but their primary goal is not supplanting one of the major parties, since New York's system allows them to acquire rewards and influence without actually winning elections on their own. First, minor parties can trade their lines and their support for patronage, usually in the form of jobs, as the Liberals received after Lindsay's reelection. Liberals reaped similar patronage rewards after the party's endorsement of Republican New York City mayoral candidate Rudolph Giuliani, who won a close race in 1993. Republicans found themselves in competition for patronage positions with Liberal party members throughout the city. Most notably, the son of the Liberal party's leader was appointed New York City's chief lobbyist in Albany (Mitchell 1993; Sack 1994).

Second, minor parties may exchange their ballot lines for ideological or policy support. The RTLP in particular is motivated by the desire to impel state lawmakers to curtail liberalized abortion practices. As party leaders have made clear, they are less interested in running their own candidates, and much more interested in endorsing major party candidates who can be persuaded to advance the right-to-life position in government in exchange for the RTLP line. The party's stated goal is to end abortions, not elect candidates (Spitzer 1987, ch. 2).

The Conservative party has also pressed ideological concerns. In 1993, for example, the state head of the Conservative party threatened Republicans in the state legislature with the withdrawal of Conservative endorsement and support if they voted for a civil rights bill aimed at protecting gays and lesbians. Support for the bill would be "close to a fatal issue" as far as party leader Michael Long was concerned (Bauder 1993). The measure failed to be enacted.

The Continued Potency of Minor Parties:
Gubernatorial and Mayoral Cases

Gubernatorial elections continue to demonstrate the attractiveness of New York's electoral system to minor parties. The 1994 gubernatorial race mentioned at the start of this chapter dramatically illustrates this point, but 1994 was no anomaly. The 1990 gubernatorial race elevated the minor party role to an even greater degree, nearly precipitating a crisis for the Republican party. The near certain reelection of Democrat Mario Cuomo deterred prominent state Republicans from challenging him. After numerous unsuccessful appeals to over twenty potential candidates, the party settled on an unknown but affluent economist, Pierre Rinfret. The Rinfret endorsement enraged the state's conservatives, who objected to his support for abortion rights and lack of conservative credentials. The Conservative party turned instead to New York University Dean Herbert London.

Rinfret proved to be an inept candidate who seemed uninformed about and uninterested in state issues. London, on the other hand, campaigned hard, and preelection polls showed the two running neck-and-neck for second place. A third-place showing for Rinfret would have been disastrous for the Republicans, as it would have reduced the party to the status of a third party, making the Conservatives the state's other major party. The Republicans would lose control over appointed patronage positions in every county in the state, and suffer a nearly incalculable loss of prestige. In the election, party loyalty prevailed, but just barely; Rinfret received 22 percent of the vote to London's 21 percent. Cuomo swept the election with 53 percent of the vote. Had Cuomo faced a single strong opponent, the race would have appeared far closer.

The 1989 and 1993 New York City mayoral contests illustrate the elasticity of minor party fortunes. After its successful endorsement of Cuomo in 1982, the Liberal party succumbed to a fierce intraparty power struggle during a time when liberalism seemed out of favor. Teetering on the edge of extinction, the Liberals came back by patching up their differences and emerging as an important force in the mayoral race. Early in 1989, Liberal party leader Raymond Harding openly courted Republican U.S. Attorney Giuliani, who had expressed interest in running for mayor. The incumbent, Ed Koch, had been no friend to liberal causes, and Harding believed that none of the other Democratic challengers could mount a strong enough challenge to defeat Koch. The link between Guiliani and the Liberals raised some eyebrows, as Giuliani's liberal credentials were less than impeccable. Although a liberal supporter of Democrat George McGovern in 1972, Giuliani had switched parties, and was appointed to his position as federal prosecutor by President Ronald Reagan. In addition, Giuliani opposed abortion and supported the death penalty. Despite the ideological compromise, the subsequent Liberal endorsement immediately made the Liberals a major player in what promised to be a close election in a crowded field. Guiliani later won the Republican nomination, making him an even more formidable challenger. And in a concession to his new-found Liberal supporters, Guiliani backtracked on some of his conservative positions, including a disavowal of his opposition to abortion. To the surprise of many, Koch was defeated in the Democratic primary by

Borough President David Dinkins, who went on to win the election by a 3 percent vote margin over Giuliani.

Liberal party leader Harding had gambled on Giuliani and lost. Nevertheless, the early endorsement signaled to Democratic leaders that the Liberals could not be ignored or taken for granted, and that they continued to exercise influence. Even Governor Cuomo's threat to shun the Liberal designation in his next race for governor if they endorsed Giuliani did not deter them. Echoing the words of party founder Alex Rose, Harding said that his party's purpose was to "keep Democrats liberal and Republicans honest" (Roberts 1989).

Four years later, the Liberal party enraged Democrats and African Americans by again endorsing Giuliani, against incumbent Mayor Dinkins (the city's first black mayor). This time, however, Giuliani won a narrow victory. As the *New York Times* noted, the race turned on "slivers of Liberal vote" (Purdum 1993). In the process, the Liberals had renewed their party, won substantial patronage, and moved a Republican closer to the liberal camp.

Conclusion

As these examples reveal, predictions of the demise of New York's minor parties are at the least premature, and at the most inaccurate. By surviving the turbulent 1980s, New York's minor parties demonstrated their staying power as well as their political flexibility. Minor and major party leaders cooperate when it is in their interest to do so. But ideological differences, personal disputes, and attempts to enhance power often turn cooperation into conflict. In examples like John Lindsay's 1969 reelection, or the 1990 gubernatorial race, the minor parties were the tail that wagged the dog.[9] But in instances like the 1986 gubernatorial campaign, the dog wagged the tail. Indeed, it would be a mistake to attribute too much influence to the minor parties. That holds true in particular for the Right-to-Life party, which has found itself in a position where major party candidates sympathetic to their point of view frequently turn down invitations to accept the RTLP endorsement because of its reputation for inflexible extremism. The RTLP also illustrates most vividly the importance of electoral structures in shaping electoral behavior. Without question, New York's cross-endorsement and party recognition rules explain the otherwise anomalous fact that one of the most strongly pro-choice states in the union is also the home of the nation's only antiabortion political party.

Finally, what does this near-multiparty system offer for the voters of New York? As previously mentioned, many major party leaders and others have come to vilify the current system (Scarrow 1983), fearing, in the extreme, political paralysis characterized by institutionalized factionalism brought about by too many parties—as occurred for example during the French Fourth Republic after World War II.[10] These fears have been heightened by the spread of single-issue politics in the 1970s and 1980s, of which the RTLP is an obvious example, and the generalized "decline of parties" (Crotty 1984). On the other hand, the New York system may offer, apart from the virtues or vices of particular parties, a feasible avenue to reinvigorate party politics by providing voters with a greater variety of party and, therefore, policy options (cf. Spitzer 1987; Mazmanian 1974). A vote for a candidate on the RTLP line, for example, is clearly an "issue vote," single issue or not. Moreover, the presence of more parties can only help diversify an electoral landscape considered by most voters to be uninteresting at best. Few could deny that the multiparty system sparks greater interest in the electoral process.

E. E. Schattschneider observed many years ago that competition was the hallmark of a vigorous party system, and that democracy was unthinkable without vigorous parties (Schattschneider 1942, 208). The current national electoral malaise leans clearly toward the side of decay and disinterest. The New York example offers a good reason to believe that party competitiveness, considered a hallmark of effective and responsive party politics, is enhanced by the presence of minor parties (Spitzer 1987). Those who complain about the woeful state of political parties in America might be well advised to give the New York system a closer look.

Notes

1. New York minor parties, and their years of official ballot status: Prohibition (1892–1922); Socialist Labor (1896–1904); Socialist (1900–38); Independent League (1906–16); Progressive (1912–16); American (1914–16); Farmer-Labor (1920–22); Law Preservation (1930–34); American Labor (1936–54); Liberal (1946–); Conservative (1962–); Right-to-Life (1978–); Independence (1994–); Freedom (1994–).

2. In 1995, for example, a Democratic-Independent candidate for Onondaga County Executive was pressured by Democrats to drop his endorsement by the RTLP. Despite the fact that the candidate faced an uphill battle against a popular Republican incumbent, the Democratic challenger agreed to drop the RTLP endorsement because Democrats had a long-standing agreement, dating from 1981, that no Democratic candidate would also accept the RTLP line (Arnold 1995).

3. The RTLP first established its ballot line in 1978 when its gubernatorial candidate, Mary Jane Tobin, received 130,193 votes.

4. Ballot position is determined by gubernatorial vote. The party whose gubernatorial candidate receives the largest vote appears first on all New York ballots, followed

by the other parties, according to the amount of gubernatorial vote. If a party does not field a gubernatorial candidate, it forfeits the line.

5. In general, New York State has the most arcane, lengthy, cumbersome, and intricate election laws of any state in the union (Oreskes 1985).

6. The first known instance of fusion was a New York gubernatorial election in 1854; at the presidential level, the first instance of fusion was in the election of 1856, when the Whigs and Know-Nothings both endorsed Millard Fillmore for president (Scarrow 1986).

7. A Minnesota law barring parties from cross-endorsing was struck down by a federal appeals court in early 1996. The case, *Timmons et al. v. Twin Cities Area New Party*, No. 95-1608, was appealed to the Supreme Court, which heard oral argument on December 4, 1996.

8. As then New York City Mayor Ed Koch noted, "I believe that the people of the state of New York are finding that the minor parties are the tail that wags the dog, and are seeking to impose their candidates on the major parties" (Hoffman 1982).

9. In Cayuga County in upstate New York, local Republicans say that "the lack of a Conservative endorsement . . . is the kiss of death to a campaign." This is true even though the local Conservative party is considered poorly organized and has a small enrollment (Hannagan 1989).

10. One symptom of the continued concern about the minor parties was seen in 1986, when the liberal *New York Times* called in an editorial for the dissolution of the Liberal party, citing its factional disputes and apparently declining influence.

Part III

Prospects

8

The Libertarian Party:
A Pragmatic Approach to Party Building

Terry Savage

In order to understand the Libertarian party's strategy one needs to be familiar with its goals and where it fits into the larger political system. Let's consider the classic political spectrum from right to left. The stereotypical person on the far right believes people should be able to keep most of their money, but that the government should regulate what they do in their personal life. So, the right wing wants to give people lots of economic freedom but less personal freedom. The stereotypical person on the far left believes people have to give up a lot of their money, but should not be regulated in their personal life. So, the left wing wants to give people less economic freedom but lots of personal freedom. Of course, these are exaggerations of real conservatives and liberals.

David Nolan, the founder of the Libertarian party, conceptualized another ideological dimension in politics. On one end is the "authoritarian" position, which wants to take all of people's money and also tell them what to do. And at the other end is the "libertarian" position, which says: you get to keep all your money and do what ever you want to do as well. So, to state it in a stereotypical form, Libertarians believe in total economic and personal freedom, so long as you don't hurt anybody else.

The situation in the United States today is pretty far from the Libertarian ideal, but a long way from when human civilization began. If you think back to when human beings were basically living in bands and tribes, there was very little liberty. The biggest, toughest, meanest guy controlled the resources and ran his neighbors' lives. As human society evolved, it moved away from this situation, following a zigzag course, first with kings and priests coming into power, and then committees and democracy, until we got to modern America, which is sort of halfway to the Libertarian ideal. People have more freedom than at the beginning, but still have a long way to go.

From this perspective, the goals of the Libertarian party are to move society toward the Libertarian ideal. However, Libertarians debate among themselves on how to realize these goals. Because of this debate, the strategy of the Libertarian party is in transition. Today there is no officially adopted document that states the strategy of the Libertarian party. I am working to create such a document for the California Libertarians, using strategic planning. It is surprisingly difficult to get some folks to recognize the need for a strategic plan because of differences in perspective.

In my view, there are two primary factions within the Libertarian party. There are the "purists" and there are the "pragmatists." The purists believe, in essence, that freedom is a natural state toward which human beings are evolving. From this perspective, all that is necessary is to remain consistent and wait for the rest of the population to catch on. The purists don't want to get involved with "politics"—all we have to do is present a clear, consistent philosophical position, and electoral victory will follow.

The pragmatists believe there are concrete steps that can be taken to move America toward the Libertarian ideal. Many of these steps are modest and they reflect the situation of the country. The Libertarian party can do more than just hold up an ideal, it can make changes in government today that can make a difference. Remember, in America today, it takes only a plurality of voters to elect someone interested in taking your money and telling you what to do. If Libertarians can participate in politics strategically, they can help the country evolve in the right direction.

The debate between the purists and the pragmatists has often been very intense. In fact, in the early to mid-1980s there was actually an agreement among the two factions not to kill each other. This meant that the purists wouldn't accuse the pragmatists of "betraying Libertarian ideals." And by the same token, pragmatists wouldn't accuse the purists of being "unrealistic." That way we could at least be civil with each other.

I understand both sides of this argument. When it comes to the ultimate goals, I'm as pure an anarchist as you can find. But when it comes to how we're going to get there, it is not going to be through hyperspace. That's not the way the world works. I expect there to be interim steps to the cosmically pure solution. I'm not sure about the time scale for this transition; it may take perhaps five to ten years.

The major political parties don't have this particular problem. The Republicans and Democrats are basically election machines. They have some sort of principles in their background that guide them sometimes. But you can't look at some concrete statement that lists the principles of the Democratic or Republican party. These parties don't have any strong principles. They're not coherent philosophically. And if you look at the way people vote, there's no strong evidence that they do so based on consistent political philosophy. This enables the major parties to win by presenting a mishmash of issues and policies.

In contrast, the Libertarian party is coherent philosophically, and that often works to our disadvantage: we have traditionally offered very consistent policies that many voters are not ready to accept. However, we are giving up this approach. When the Libertarian party was formed in 1971, it was made up of very committed ideological folks and it was 100 percent purist. After twenty-five years, we have elected a handful of local candidates and just one state legislator in California. Partly because of these failures, but also because of the taste of success, the number of purists has declined to the point where in 1996 the party was about 50 percent purist. Thus there is a very, very close balance between the purists and the pragmatists. I predict that this trend will continue, with the proportion of purists continuing to drop and the proportion of pragmatists continuing to increase. For example, Harry Browne, the 1996 Libertarian presidential nominee, is a pragmatist.

A new strategy is emerging among Libertarians and it has three pieces. The first, and probably the most significant, piece is to wake up and smell the coffee about the importance of money in politics. We've long believed that because our ideas are right, people will eventually catch on to them and we'll be elected because of our intellectual merit. That is nonsense. Libertarians have to run effective, well-financed campaigns to win.

My experience serves as an example. When I ran for the state legislature the campaign dominated my life for a year. I raised $55,000, the most money a Libertarian had ever raised in California. I also campaigned intensively, talking to everyone I could, and I got great media attention. I received 7 percent of the vote, about double what Libertarians normally get. I'm very proud of this campaign, but I simply did not have the money to compete effectively.

Along these lines, I think it was a mistake for Browne to turn down federal matching funds in the presidential race. It was for philosophical reasons, of course, which I understand. But the funds could have helped the presidential campaign and indirectly the campaigns of other Libertarians. In fact, a good indicator of the ascendance of the pragmatists will be when the party accepts federal matching funds. That may not happen by the year 2000, but I predict that in every election from 2004 on, the Libertarian candidate will take matching funds.

The second piece of the new strategy is to realize that campaigns need to be aimed at persuading people to vote for our candidate. Overall, there are currently few real Libertarians in the electorate. As I pointed out before, most people are part of a giant blob in the middle of the ideological perspective. In fact, about 99.9 percent of the voters are there. Most of these people don't look at the Libertarian party as a possibility; most of them see us as a bunch of nuts. So if we are going to win elections, we have to start where the people are.

It has been a slow, painful process for Libertarians to realize that the party can't present voters with purist issue positions that they oppose and still win elections. In retrospect, a purist approach was a stupid one, but it wasn't obvious to people who had very strong philosophical beliefs and were convinced they were right. But to the average voter, Libertarian positions are ideas that they have to choose over other ideas that may seem equally plausible. Libertarians need to discuss issues voters care about and stress Libertarian solutions that people find acceptable even if the positions are less than our ultimate goals. Persuading people is the key to winning elections.

The third piece of the new strategy is focusing our resources where they will do the most good. Here we have a chicken-and-egg problem: many people won't support Libertarian candidates because we aren't electing anybody. I did an analysis for the 1994 election, and the whole amount of money spent by the state party on all candidates was probably enough to elect one assembly candidate. Assembly races typically cost between $200,000 and $250,000 in California. If we want to succeed, we can't spread our resources too thin. If we focus our resources on one or two seats, we might actually win them.

Winning is absolutely critical. Once we elect people to the assembly, an irreversible change in public perception will occur. First, it will become clear to voters that Libertarians are a possibility, and in addition, Libertarians in office can develop good records to show voters. They can be the swing votes in the legislatures where the major parties are fairly evenly balanced, such as in California. In fact, in my 1994 race, the vote I received was essentially the difference between the Republican and Democratic candidates. The Democrat won the race and the local Republicans to this day blame me for keeping Willie Brown as speaker of the California Assembly. They believe the Republican would have won had I not been in the race, and that with one more vote, the Republicans would have controlled the assembly. In the Nevada legislature, the state assembly is currently split 21 to 21 between the Democrats and Republicans. Suppose it was 20 to 20 with two Libertarians, then the Libertarians could make a big difference. And it is much easier to gain this kind of influence in Nevada, where assembly districts have 15,000 registered voters as opposed to 180,000 in California. The winning candidates for state assembly in Nevada typically spend less than I did in my losing race in California.

So the goal of the party is to move American society toward the Libertarian ideal. A pragmatic strategy will hasten that day and it will have three components: (1) raising enough money to be competitive, (2) discussing issues in a sensible manner, and (3) focusing resources where they can make a difference.

9

The Reform Party:
An Issue-Driven Awakening

Justin A. Roberts

The Reform party is the new kid on the block in terms of political parties in California and the nation. So we are just beginning to confront many of the problems that other minor parties have been dealing with for years. When people ask "What are the goals and strategies of the Reform party," I respond by asking: "What day of the week is it?" The odyssey of the party began on September 25, 1996, with Ross Perot's announcement on the *Larry King Live* show. To say that the party is still evolving is an understatement!

To understand the goals and strategies of the Reform party, one must go back to 1992 and examine the issues that energized Perot's presidential campaign. Remember what the major party candidates were ignoring? Federal budget deficits and the national debt. Perot brought those issues to the fore in the 1992 presidential election and they dominated debates in the 103rd and 104th Congresses. In 1996, the country is one trillion dollars deeper in debt and a balanced budget still eludes the legislative and executive branches of the federal government.

After the 1992 campaign, Perot founded United We Stand America (UWSA), a nonprofit, nonpartisan issues advocacy organization, to keep the issues of fiscal responsibility and governmental reform on the front burner of American politics. Over time, I and many others active in UWSA began to recognize that the organization had one significant shortcoming: its nonprofit status precluded candidate endorsements. Indeed, some Perot supporters disagreed with the concept of UWSA and in 1993 started political party formation in several states. The Independence party of New York, American party of Oregon, and Patriot parties in several states are examples.

After the 1994 elections, as political gridlock gripped Washington, D.C., a consensus was developing within the UWSA organization that the time may be ripe for a new centrist political party. UWSA members and staff catalogued the Byzantine party formation rules that existed in all fifty states. By the spring of 1995, I had participated in forming a new party task force for UWSA-California to do preliminary planning to implement in my state any national new party movement. Finally, a three-day national conference was held in Dallas in August that was attended by over five thousand UWSA activists. Candidates for the Republican presidential nomination, House and Senate majority and minority leaders, and the chairmen of the Republican and Democratic National Committees addressed the conference. President Bill Clinton was invited but did not attend.

I viewed the Dallas conference as the major parties' last chance to convince a group of concerned citizens that the two major parties were capable of confronting and solving our country's major problems. Most conference attendees apparently were not convinced. It has been reported that over 70 percent of the UWSA members participating in conference workshops favored forming a new political party.

California was pivotal to the Reform party movement. California's ballot access deadline was October 24, 1995, the earliest in the nation for the 1996 election cycle. There was a concern that if ballot access failed in the most populous state with the most electoral votes, new party enthusiasm would diminish or disappear in other states. The task of registering 89,007 voters in the Reform party in less than one month seemed daunting, but incredible efforts by hundreds of volunteers resulted in 124,000 registrations by the deadline. Previously, no political party had ever gained ballot access in California in less than two years.

Buoyed by success in California, the Reform party gained ballot access or Perot qualified as an independent candidate in all fifty states and the District of Columbia. The incredible energy that made this effort possible is generated by Reform party members' commitment on issues. The national debt, federal budget deficits, the trade deficit, campaign finance reform, lobbying reform, and term limits are core issues on the Reform party agenda (see "Principles of Reform" below). Many of us believe that the country faces long-term economic and social decline unless there are major structural changes in our political system. The present major political parties are dominated by their inability to tackle tough problems and solve them. Their track record has provided the impetus for this new party movement. Reform party supporters are angry and frustrated, but they are not radical. They have simply put out a call for politics to return to a common-sense center point in the political spectrum.

The Reform Party: Principles of Reform

The following are the Principles of Reform that Ross Perot and other candidates of the Reform Party pledge to follow. They were created by the attendees of the United We Stand America National Conference held in August, 1995. Party platforms will adhere to these principles. These are designed to focus attention on the government and economic reforms that this Party and the majority of Americans want accomplished.

- High Ethical Standards for the White House and Congress
    Set the highest ethical standards for the White House and Congress.
    No more gifts.
    No more trips or junkets paid for by special interests.
    No more free meals.
    Pass laws with significant penalties—not rules.
    Give Congress and the White House the same retirement and health care plans as the average citizen.

- Balance the Budget
    Develop a detailed blue print to balance the budget.
    Eliminate the practice of keeping some programs off-budget.
    Pass the Balanced Budget Amendment.
    Create an annual financial report in plain language so the American people will know whether or not we are following the plan to balance the budget.

- Campaign Reform
    Reduce the cost of campaigns by shortening the election cycle to no more than four months.
    Hold elections on Saturdays and Sundays—Not Tuesdays—So working people can get to the polls.
    Replace the Electoral College process for electing the President with a direct vote from the citizens—so that every vote counts.
    Prohibit announcements of exit polls until all voting has been completed in Hawaii.
    Require Members of Congress to raise all campaign funds from the voters in their district.
    Require members of the Senate to raise all campaign funds from the voters in their state.

- Term Limits

    Limit Members of Congress to three terms in the House of Representatives.

    Limit Senators to two terms in the Senate.

    The new tax system must be fair.

    The new tax system must be paperless.

    The new tax system must raise the money required to pay the bills.

    Require that any future tax increases under the new system be approved by the people in the next federal election, in order to impose discipline on spending.

- Medicare, Medicaid, and Social Security

    Carefully put together plans to deal with Medicare, Medicaid and Social Security.

    Explain these plans in detail to the American People.

    Get a consensus.

    Pilot test each of these programs before implementing them nationwide to make sure they produce the anticipated results at the anticipated costs.

    Keep these programs dynamic, so they can be changed based on experience. Don't freeze them with restrictive legislation.

- Lobbying Restrictions

    Elected officials, appointees and all employees of the Legislative and Executive Branches come to serve, not "Cash in."

    Prohibit former elected and appointed officials from ever taking money from foreign governments or foreign interests. The current practice sends a terrible signal to current and future officeholders. It causes them to build relationships with foreign interests and foreign governments at the expenses of the U.S. taxpayer.

- Foreign Lobbying

    Prohibit any former federal employees—including elected officials—from working as a domestic lobbyist for five years after leaving government service.

    Foreign countries can provide information to our government through the State and Commerce Department and the Executive Branch, but cannot give contributions or gifts of any kind.

Foreign representatives can visit with Members of Congress, but under no circumstances can they give them anything now or later.

- Domestic Lobbying

  Prohibit any former federal employees—including elected officials—from working as a domestic lobbyist for five years after leaving government service.

  Limit domestic lobbying to presenting client's ideas to the Legislative and Executive Branches.

  Prohibit domestic lobbyists from giving money, trips or other incentives to current or former members of the Legislative and Executive Branches.

- Create Jobs in the USA

  Negotiate trade agreements that promote American jobs, consumer safety, environmental protection, and fair trade.

  Create a business environment that supports small business, which accounts for roughly 80 percent of jobs held by Americans today. Trade agreements, tax reform, and other programs must reflect the needs of small business.

10

The Green Party: Global Politics at the Grassroots

Greg Jan

Like other minor parties, the Green party also has a consistent philosophical position. Greens are deeply concerned with the environment
but their understanding of it is in a larger sense for the whole natural
world. This understanding can be summarized to some extent with the
term "sustainability"—an economy that is sustainable, a society that
is sustainable, and even a culture that is sustainable. Most Greens have
a strong critique, of course, not only of the environmental situation,
but of the broader social and economic order. So much in the world is
not sustainable. We are depleting our natural resources and causing all
sorts of pollution, and that simply cannot continue. Exponential growth
curves show that within the next ten to fifty to perhaps one hundred
years, people are going to have to make enormous changes in the way
we are living, not only across the United States, but all over the whole
planet. And that implies a lot of changes in all aspects of human life,
including political changes.

The long-term goals of the Greens are to get us to a point where
we can live in a manner that sustains life on the planet and human
civilization. It is confusing to go about our daily lives with the general
knowledge that this enormous change is necessary and inevitable, yet
see our society make very little progress in that direction from day to
day and year to year. Nevertheless, most Greens have accepted some
kind of middle-term goals that are consistent with the long-term goal
of sustainability and that contribute to the enormous changes necessary
to achieve it. For example, most Greens accept the need to educate the
public on the problems facing the planet and to present possible solutions. At the same time, Greens hope to gain credibility and respect, so
that others will recognize the problems we identify, and accept that we
have a reasonable approach in solving them.

Our strategies to achieve these goals are quite diverse, but can
be divided into two basic stages. The first might be called the "pre-

electoral" stage, which lasted from about 1984 to 1990 and preceded the formation of political party committees linked to the Green movement. The second might be called the "political party" stage, from 1991 to the present. The pre-electoral stage gave Greens lots of credibility in local communities because of the local projects we accomplished. The party stage has given the movement a chance to translate that credibility into government. All told, we now hold twenty-nine elected offices in the country. And of course, with Ralph Nader as our presidential candidate in 1996, even more people learned about the Green party.

The Green movement started in Germany in 1979–80 as a coalition of people from environmental, peace, and social justice movement backgrounds. Because of the proportional representation system in West Germany, they thought they had a strong opening to compete in elections, and they were quite successful. By 1983, the party had achieved the minimal threshold for seats in the German parliament. This success sent shock waves across the whole planet. Green parties spread quickly throughout Western Europe, and eventually to Australia, Latin America, and Africa.

In this country, Charlene Spretnak and Fritjof Capra, two local authors in the San Francisco Bay area, wrote the book *Green Politics*, published in 1984, which discussed these developments and how they might spread to the United States. Because of the success of the book, a kind of founding meeting was held in Minneapolis in late 1984, where the American Green movement was created. At that time it was called the Committees of Correspondence after the group that preceded the American Revolution.

Two very important decisions came out of this meeting. The first was to expand the four founding principles of the German Green party—ecology, nonviolence, social justice, and grassroots democracy—into ten key values. The committee added significant emphasis on local community activity, such as community-based economics and decentralization.

The other decision was that individuals should go back to their own local areas, form local groups, and find ways to tap the energy of the local people. This decentralization was to be held together by an informal national structure, a national clearinghouse, and national meetings of representatives from local areas to share information and develop plans. So, the first strategy of the party was to go back to the grassroots areas, to form local groups, to emphasize education and publicity, and to undertake local projects.

During this pre-electoral stage, Green groups formed all over the United States, but they were especially strong on the West Coast, in New England, and in the upper Midwest. These groups focused on local projects, many of which were not political in the electoral sense of the word, but they created strong grassroots support for the Green movement. National meetings, starting in 1987 and becoming annual events since 1989, kept these local efforts connected to one another. An important effect of these pre-electoral activities was a kind of translating of what was happening around the globe to America at the local level. Obviously, the name Green had a strong impact, not only because it represented ecology and the views coming from ecology, but also because people recognized it as a strong political force from all over the planet and identified with its values.

In these early days, the Green movement was not involved in electoral politics, with small exceptions in Wisconsin and Connecticut. Most Greens emphasized their local projects and local education. But gradually many people realized there was a limit to how much could be accomplished by these nonelectoral means. So a number of state groups started talking about getting involved in elections and campaigns.

The first Green party to achieve ballot status was in Alaska in 1990. Then, in 1992, parties in California, Arizona, Hawaii, and New Mexico achieved ballot access, followed by Maine and Colorado. A number of other states also started Green parties, but because their ballot access laws were a little more challenging or because the Greens were a little less organized in those areas, they didn't achieve ballot status. These states include Missouri, Rhode Island, Virginia, Wisconsin, and North Carolina.

In this second political party stage, a critical part of the strategy was to do well in elections. However, we were not expecting to win partisan elections immediately. One plan was to focus on races in small states where it costs less to run campaigns, and we actually did quite well in a number of places. For example, in Hawaii in 1994, we received 40 percent in one state legislature race, and many of our candidates won over 10 percent of the vote. We were able to create a lot of attention, getting publicity not only for our candidates, but also for the goals of the Green parties.

In the meantime, in the larger states, particularly California, which was the only large ballot-qualified state at that time, we knew it was going to be very difficult to do well in partisan races. So we didn't actually put a lot of effort into those races. We did have a number of candidates, especially in 1992, that ran more out of personal interest than as part of a collective strategy at the state level.

A more successful statewide effort was in New Mexico in 1994, when a former Democratic lieutenant governor, Roberto Mondragon, changed to the Green party because he strongly identified with us, and ran for governor. This was a conscious strategy to take the awareness of the Green party to a new level. The campaign did very well, getting just over 10 percent of the vote. I think that perhaps more than anywhere else people in New Mexico are now very much aware of the Greens, and Mondragon ran for the state legislature in 1996. I think we'll have a good chance soon of bringing our first Green into a state legislature office. Of course, the 1996 presidential year and Ralph Nader gave us an even greater opportunity to get our message out and gain credibility and respect. We had fairly strong Green parties organized in thirty to forty states.

There are, however, real limits to the strategy of running national and statewide candidates because we are not in a position to win at these levels. Greens quickly recognized that we should also put our efforts and resources into local races where we could actually have a chance of winning. Once our candidates are in office, we can start implementing Green positions and philosophies in local government, and develop our own credibility. For instance, in California we now have at least sixteen Greens elected to local office; several others have been elected in other states. We expect the number of viable local Green candidates to increase steadily in the years ahead.

The shift from the pre-electoral to the political party stage has generated some discussion among Greens. Because of these electoral successes, more and more Greens are seeing the advantages of a political party strategy. These people tend to take a more pragmatic view toward educating the public and implementing the Green agenda, if only a step at a time. However, it is important to note that not all Greens endorse this strategy; there are still some people across the country that remain more focused on their local activities, such as co-ops or organic gardening projects. Some simply don't care for electoral activities, while others feel there is a great danger in losing the focus of the movement.

There is also another kind of electoral strategy that many Greens are pursuing: to support the move for proportional representation in elections. Greens are supporting the Center for Voting and Democracy in Washington, D.C., the major advocacy group spreading the idea of proportional representation across the country. And in San Francisco, there was an election in November 1996 to change the San Francisco Board of Supervisors to give the voters the opportunity to change that election system from an at-large system—where the top vote-getters win—to a transferable voting system that will include a form of proportional representation. However, in contrast, Greens have generally been against another alternative electoral strategy, "fusion," where Greens endorse other parties' candidates. The saying is "fusion is confusion" because it inevitably dilutes the Green message.

The central purpose of the party strategy is to keep the Green critique and the solutions that flow from it before the public so that we can alter the direction of American society. Successful electoral activity helps educate the public on the problems facing the planet, which we believe will have to be confronted in some fashion or another in the near future. Other gains can be made by contesting elections. Policies can be altered and resources redirected to address real solutions. This can take place by having Greens elected to office, by having other parties co-opt our ideas, or perhaps by changing the representation system.

As we look to the future, most Greens believe that our local non-electoral and electoral efforts will contribute to having the country confront the global and national problems before it, and help move us toward a sustainable society. In this sense, the Green party is the embodiment of a well-known saying, "think globally, act locally."

11

Institutional Obstacles to a Multiparty System

Richard Winger

Contrary to what most people believe, minor parties in the United States do sometimes win partisan elections. Over the past fifty years, these victories have been concentrated in certain states. The thesis of this chapter is that minor parties win elections in states with favorable election laws and that they don't win elections in states with unfavorable laws. To demonstrate this point, I will correlate key characteristics of state election law with the historical record on minor party victories.

Why does it matter if minor parties win elections? Minor parties are an important part of the two-party system, giving voice to ideological minorities and fostering communication between them and the major parties. Thus minor parties help legitimize the electoral process. Those of us who worry about low voter turnout, and the millions of U.S. citizens who stay at home because they feel unrepresented, should be interested in healthy minor parties. The possibility of victory and an occasional win at the polls helps foster healthy minor parties. Of course, minor party victories are rare even under favorable laws, since there are many other factors that are required for electoral success. But unfavorable state laws put an unwarranted burden on one of the most dynamic elements of the political process, minor parties.

Minor Party Victories Since 1945

Table 11.1 lists states in which minor parties have won partisan elections for federal or state office since the end of World War II (the District of Columbia is treated as a state).[1] Table 11.2 lists states in which minor parties have won partisan elections for local office. Table 11.2 is not comprehensive: it lists up to three cases of local minor party victories per state, even though there may have been more cases in such states.

Table 11.1
Minor Party Victories in Federal or State Offices Since 1945

State	Year	Party	Offices Won
Alaska	1978	Libertarian	State representative
Alaska	1980	Libertarian	Two state representatives
Alaska	1984	Libertarian	State representative
Alaska	1990	Alaska Ind.	Governor and lieutenant governor
Alaska	1992	Alaska Ind.	State representative
Connecticut	1990	A Conn.	Governor and lieutenant governor
New Hampshire	1992	Libertarian	Four state representatives
New Hampshire	1994	Libertarian	Two state representatives
New York	1948	Amer. Labor	Two U.S. House members
New York	1949	Liberal	One U.S. House member
New York	1970	Conservative	U.S. senator
Tennessee	1970	American	State senator
Vermont	1992	Prog. Coal.	Two state representatives
Vermont	1994	Prog. Coal.	One state representative
Vermont	1996	Prog. Coal.	Three state representatives

Since 1945, minor parties have won elections for federal or state office in six states. They elected governors and lieutenant governors in Alaska and Connecticut, and three U.S. members of Congress and one U.S. senator in New York. Minor parties in Alaska, New Hampshire, Tennessee, and Vermont have all elected members of the state legislature. In fifteen states, minor parties have won partisan local offices, including mayors, county commissioners, and members of city, county, and township councils. Combining the two tables produces a list of eighteen states. There are thus thirty-three states where minor parties have not won in the past half-century.

What do these eighteen states have in common? There is no obvious regional factor. Four are in the West, four in the Midwest, three in the South, and seven in the East. Nor is there an obvious economic or ethnic factor. The list includes wealthy (Connecticut) and poor (Alabama) states, farming (Kansas) and industrial (New Jersey) states. It also includes states with very few ethnic minorities (Idaho, New Hampshire) and states with substantial ethnic minority populations (Texas, New York, Hawaii). The thirty-three states where minor parties have not won are equally diverse.

Table 11.2
Minor Party Victories for Local Office Since 1945

State	Year	Party	Offices Won
Alabama	1988	Libertarian	Constable, Lee County
Alabama	1994	Patriot	County commissioner, Greene County
Connecticut	1945	Socialist	Mayor, Bridgeport
Connecticut	1947	Socialist	Mayor, Bridgeport
Connecticut	1947	Socialist	Mayor, South Norwalk
Dist. Columbia	1974	Statehood	City council-at-large
Dist. Columbia	1978	Statehood	City council-at-large
Dist. Columbia	1982	Statehood	City council-at-large
Hawaii	1992	Green	Hawaii County Council
Hawaii	1994	Green	Hawaii County Council
Idaho	1976	American	Sheriff, Teton County
Indiana	1950	Prohibition	4 township officials, Harrison County
Indiana	1959	Prohibition	2 town councilmen, Winona Lake
Kansas	1948	Prohibition	11 township officials, Jewell County
Kansas	1950	Prohibition	19 township officials, Cloud, Jewell and Sherman Counties
Kansas	1952	Prohibition	Sheriff, Jewell County
Michigan	1972	Human Rts.	2 city councilmen, Ann Arbor
Michigan	1974	Human Rts.	City councilman, Ann Arbor
Michigan	1996	Libertarian	2 township officials, Washtenaw County
New Jersey	1981	Libertarian	Township official, Hunterdon County
New York	1945	Communist	2 city councilmen, New York City
New York	1969	Liberal	Mayor, New York City
New York	1979	Rt. to Life	Supervisor, Cheektowaga
Pennsylvania	1981	Libertarian	Township Official, Union County
Pennsylvania	1993	Patriot	School board, Allegheny County
Pennsylvania	1993	Libertarian	Township official, Clarion County
Texas	1970	La Raza Unida	County commissioner, LaSalle County
Texas	1972	La Raza Unida	5 County officials, Zavala County
Texas	1974	La Raza Unida	6 County officials, Zavala County
Utah	1987	Libertarian	Mayor and 2 councilmen, Bigwater
Utah	1988	Libertarian	3 City councilmen, Bigwater
Utah	1989	Libertarian	Mayor and 2 councilmen, Bigwater
Vermont	1982	Libertarian	High bailiff, Grand Isle County
Vermont	1982	Citizens	2 aldermen, Burlington
Vermont	1983	Citizens	2 aldermen, Burlington
Wisconsin	1982	Libertarian	Coroner, Iowa County

The Impact of State Laws

There are, however, important differences in state election laws that distinguish the eighteen states with minor party success from the other thirty-three states. What follows is a discussion of the five most important features of state law in this regard.

Parties Can Nominate Recent Converts

The states with minor party victories allow a political party to nominate any citizen that otherwise meets the constitutional qualifications to hold the office and has not lost the primary of some other party for that same office that year. By contrast, some of the states in which minor parties never win make it illegal for minority parties to nominate people who have not been party members for very long. The most restrictive states are California, Oklahoma, Colorado, and Kentucky, and as a result of 1995 legislation, Nevada and New Mexico.

California and Oklahoma do not permit any political party to appear on the general election ballot unless that party nominates all its candidates in the primary election. California provides that no one may enter a partisan primary unless he or she has been a registered member of that party for at least three months and has not been a member of any *other* qualified party at any time during the preceding year. Oklahoma does not permit anyone to enter a primary unless that individual has been a registered member of that party for the preceding six months. An exception is made in both states for the first elections in which a party participates.

Colorado defines a "political party" to be an organization that polled at least 10 percent for governor, a definition so strict that no minor party has been a "party" in Colorado since 1916. Consequently, minor party candidates can only obtain a spot on the Colorado ballot by using the independent candidate petition procedure, which permits the candidate a partisan label, as long as the label is not similar to "Democrat" or "Republican." Colorado does not accept the petition of any independent candidate who was registered as a Republican or Democrat during the year before the petition deadline. Like Colorado, Kentucky has no procedure for a new party to qualify as a "party" until after it has polled a certain share of the vote. Consequently, minor party candidates generally qualify by using the independent candidate petition method. Kentucky won't accept independent candidate petitions if the candidate was a member of a qualified party at any time after November of the year before the election.

Nevada, where minor parties nominate by convention, does not permit a minor party to nominate anyone who has changed his or her party membership since September 1 of the year preceding the election. New Mexico, where minor parties generally nominate by convention, does not permit such conventions to nominate anyone who was not a member by January 31 of the election year.

Laws that forbid minor parties from nominating anyone who was a member of the Democratic or Republican party, for as long as a year or more before an election (the Colorado period is eighteen months), severely limit the ability of minor parties to win elections. Minor parties generally have the best chance of winning when they choose well-known candidates. And the types of people who are well known in politics have almost always been members of the Democratic or Republican party until shortly before they were invited to be a minor party nominee.

A good example of this situation is Roberto Mondragon, Green party candidate for governor of New Mexico in 1994, who had been a popular Democratic lieutenant governor. As the Green party candidate, he polled over 10 percent of the vote in 1994, not enough to win, but enough to give the Green party a foothold in the state. Mondragon didn't change his registration from "Democrat" to "Green" until July 1994. Current law that year, as interpreted by the New Mexico supreme court in *Madrid v. Gonzales*, didn't bar the Greens from nominating Mondragon, despite his newcomer status to the party. But in 1995 the New Mexico legislature, controlled by Democrats who were angry that the Mondragon candidacy seemed to cost the Democrats the gubernatorial election, changed the law to add time restrictions.

In 1990, two minor party candidates won gubernatorial elections: Lowell Weicker formed A Connecticut party and won on its ticket; Walter Hickel accepted the nomination of the previously qualified Alaska Independence party and won on that ticket. Both had been registered Republicans as recently as the beginning of the year. If Alaska and Connecticut had forbidden minor parties from nominating candidates who had recently been registered members of a major party, neither victory could have occurred. Clearly, severe restrictions on the ability of minor parties to nominate recent converts hurt their ability to win elections.

A few additional states have more moderate time restrictions on minor party nominees: Maine and Massachusetts forbid minor parties from nominating candidates who have been registered members of major parties for the preceding three months. Pennsylvania has a one-month restriction, which is imposed only on minor parties that did not poll as much as 2 percent of the winning candidate's vote in the previous election.

Fusion Is Legal

"Fusion" means that it is legal for two parties to jointly nominate the same candidate (if both the parties and the candidate consent) and the candidate's name appears on the ballot under both parties' names. Arkansas, Connecticut, New Hampshire, New York, South Carolina, South Dakota, Utah, and Vermont permitted fusion between major and minor parties during the 1996 election. As a result of 1996 decisions in the Third and Eighth Circuits of the federal courts, fusion is permitted in Delaware, Iowa, Minnesota, Missouri, Nebraska, New Jersey, North Dakota, and Pennsylvania, but these decisions are so recent that they have not yet had any practical effect in any election. Fusion is prohibited in the other states.

Many advocates of fusion talk in terms of only minor party cross-nominating a major party candidate. The truth is that fusion is even more valuable to minor parties when *minor party members* capture their own party's nomination as well as the nomination of one of the major parties. This is how all the Libertarians elected to the New Hampshire legislature in 1992 and 1994 succeeded. They were all registered Libertarians, they all won the Libertarian nomination, but they also all won the Democratic or Republican nomination by write-in votes in the respective primaries.

If fusion were legal in more states, minor parties would probably be better represented in elected office. In 1994, a Libertarian party candidate for a Delaware legislative seat also won the Republican nomination for the same seat. However, a state Attorney General Opinion was hastily prepared, stating that the candidate could not be the nominee of both parties. This, of course, greatly diminished his chances of winning the general election.

There are great opportunities for minor party members to win their own party's nomination and to win a major party nomination as well when fusion is permitted. Consistently, one or the other of the major parties runs no one at all for 35 percent of all state legislative seats. Obviously, when no one else is running in a major party primary, it's very easy for a minor party candidate, nominated by his or her own party, to also win the nomination of one of the major parties by default if fusion is permitted.

The U.S. Supreme Court heard oral arguments on December 4, 1996, in *Timmons et al. v. Twin Cities Area New Party*, to settle the question of whether the First Amendment's free association language requires states to permit fusion, at least when both political parties and the candidate all wish to do so. (See the introduction to this volume for a discussion of the resolution of this case.)

Ballot Access Requirements Are Lenient

The ballot access laws differ tremendously from state to state. Not surprisingly, minor parties are much more likely to win elections when such laws are lenient. In some states, ballot access is relatively easy. For example, several states grant automatic ballot access to parties that polled enough votes in the previous election. But in other states, a minor party may need to spend several hundred thousand dollars just to get on the ballot.

The leniency of ballot access for minor parties is very difficult to measure.[2] Basically, it is a function of two variables: (1) How difficult is it to *get* the party on the ballot? (2) How difficult is it for the party to *remain* on the ballot?

The difficulty of getting on the ballot is a function not only of how many signatures are required on a petition, but of how many different petitions a party needs to circulate. In most states, a single petition qualifies a new minor party for the ballot for all partisan offices. But in twelve states a separate petition is required for each legislative and U.S. House candidate. It is far more difficult to circulate a separate petition for each candidate than it is to circulate a single statewide petition. Petition due dates also vary, ranging from the October in the year before the election to the September of an election year. The amount of time permitted for circulating the petition also varies. There are other variables, such as whether petitions must be notarized, whether only registered voters may sign, and whether the petition must be circulated only in certain periods of time.

The difficulty of remaining on the ballot is also complicated. Alabama requires a party to poll 20 percent in the previous election in order to be on the ballot automatically for the next election. By contrast, South Carolina merely requires a party to run at least one candidate every four years in order to stay on the ballot. Most states permit the vote of any of a minor party's candidates to "count" toward the goal of remaining on the ballot but a substantial minority of states provide that only a single office, such as president or governor, "counts" toward that goal. Because minor parties generally poll many more votes for unimportant statewide offices, such as treasurer or secretary of state, than they do for president or governor, minor parties are much better off in a state in which any statewide vote counts toward the goal of retaining a spot on the ballot.

Furthermore, the number of statewide offices varies greatly from state to state. Alaska, Hawaii, Maine, New Hampshire, and New Jersey do not elect any statewide state offices, except for governor (or a team of governor and lieutenant governor). By contrast, some states elect as many as a dozen statewide state partisan officers in a single election. Obviously, if a minor party can retain its spot on the ballot by polling 3 percent of the vote for any statewide office, its chances of remaining on the ballot are far higher in a state that elects twelve such offices versus a state with only two or three.

Even the ballot format affects a party's ability to remain on the ballot. The tendency of voters to be more generous with their votes for minor party candidates for less important statewide office, such as auditor, than they are willing to vote for a more important office (such as president or governor) is dampened in states with a "party circle device" or "party lever" on the ballot. These devices permit a voter to cast a vote for all partisan offices with a single flick of the wrist if the voter is interested in voting for the entire ticket of just one particular party. In the states with such a device, the vote for minor party candidates for less important office, while still bigger than the vote for the top-of-the-ticket candidates, is only moderately bigger.

Because of all these difficulties, here we adopt a simple objective test to determine the leniency of ballot access laws. Such laws are deemed to be "lenient" if there was at least one minor party candidate on the ballot for some federal or state office, in *all* elections, for the period 1946–96. A state's law is labeled "moderate" if there was at least one minor party candidate on the ballot in at least *half* of all elections in the state for the same period. And if there wasn't a single minor party candidate on the ballot in more than half of all election years in 1946–96, that state's law is deemed "severe."[3] This classification is useful, although it does not reflect changes in the state law. For example, Mississippi and Oregon are in the severe category above, but their laws became more lenient during the 1990s.

By this measure nine states have lenient ballot access laws: Colorado, Connecticut, Massachusetts, Minnesota, New Jersey, New York, Pennsylvania, Washington, and Wisconsin.

Twenty-three states and the District of Columbia have moderate ballot access laws: Alabama, Alaska, Arizona, California, Delaware, Hawaii, Idaho, Illinois, Indiana, Iowa, Kansas, Kentucky, Michigan, Missouri, Montana, Nevada, New Hampshire, New Mexico, Rhode Island, South Carolina, Texas, Utah, and Vermont.

The remaining eighteen states have severe ballot access laws: Arkansas, Florida, Georgia, Louisiana, Maine, Maryland, Mississippi, Nebraska, North Carolina, North Dakota, Ohio, Oklahoma, Oregon, South Dakota, Tennessee, Virginia, West Virginia, and Wyoming.

Some state ballot access laws are so severe that minor party candidates simply cannot get on the ballot. Florida has had only two minor party candidates for Congress, and only seventeen candidates for the state legislature, on the ballot in the past seventy years. Georgia has had only seven minor party candidates on the ballot for the state legislature in the past fifty years. Arkansas, Maryland, and Tennessee have not had any minor party candidates on the ballot for the state legislature since 1970. West Virginia has had only three minor party candidates on the ballot for the state legislature since 1936. Louisiana has had only one minor party candidate on the ballot for the state legislature since 1971. Not surprisingly, only once has a minor party won a partisan election in a state with severe ballot access laws.

Internal Nomination Procedures Are Reasonable

In almost all states, once a minor party gets the coveted status of "qualified political party," it is free to nominate as many candidates as it wishes, without too much difficulty. But in a few states, even if a party gains "qualified" status, it finds itself virtually unable to nominate any candidates. This factor explains why there has been so few minor party candidates in Maine, a state that, politically, seems ripe for minor party success.

Maine voters elected an independent governor in 1974 and again in 1994. In 1992 Ross Perot polled more votes than Republican nominee George Bush in Maine, and in 1996 Maine was again Perot's best state. Therefore, one would think that the Green and Reform parties, both of which are fully qualified parties in Maine, ought to be in a position to run some winning campaigns. The fact is that Maine law prevented the Green and Reform parties from having candidates for any office on the ballot in 1996 except for the presidency. Maine has stiff petition requirements for any candidate to win a place on his or her own party's primary ballot, which are especially demanding for minor parties because they do not take into account the size of the party. By law, anyone who wishes to be on the primary ballot for statewide office must obtain 2,000 signatures of registered party members. The Green party has only about 3,000 registered members in Maine, and it is onerous to collect 2,000 signatures from an eligible pool of 3,000 people who are scattered across an entire state. The Reform party has about 23,000 registered members in Maine, but even it was unable to field any candidates in its own primary, and yet there are literally no candidates on those primary ballots. Furthermore, minor party primary voters can't even use the write-in method for candidates in the primaries because write-in ballots only count if the total matches or exceeds the 2,000 signatures required on a primary petition.

The only other state with a similar election law problem is Massachusetts. In 1996, the Libertarian party was the only fully qualified minor party in that state, and except for two candidates for the state legislature, it was unable to run any candidates in its own direct primary because it had only about 9,000 registered members, and 10,000 signatures were needed to place a candidate on the ballot for statewide offices that year. Massachusetts permits a candidate seeking a place on his or her party's primary ballot to obtain signatures of party members and also registered independents, so the Massachusetts law isn't as severe as the Maine law, but it still constitutes a hurdle for minor parties.

The irony of the Maine and Massachusetts restrictions is that minor parties that have won a fair degree of voter support have more difficult ballot access problems than minor parties that have not won much voter support. It is easier for an unqualified minor party to run candidates in Maine and Massachusetts than it is for a qualified minor party. When a minor party is unqualified in Maine or Massachusetts, it can obtain the signature of any registered voter on petitions. Only after the party has shown enough voter support to qualify for "party" status and its own primary does it lose the right to collect signatures from all registered voters. Both state laws have been upheld in lower federal courts. The laws governing party nominations help explain why minor parties have not won elections in either Maine or Massachusetts in the past fifty years despite minor party appeal and activity in both places.

The nomination laws of Georgia and Illinois also hinder minor party success. In these states, a minor party that gains "qualified party" status for statewide office may not have such status for district and county office. In Illinois, a party that polls 5 percent for any statewide race is entitled to nominate candidates for statewide office with its own closed primary. However, such a party is *not* "qualified" for district or county office, and if it wishes to run candidates for legislative or local office, it must submit separate petitions signed by 5 percent of the previous general election vote cast for that office. Only if the party polled 5 percent for governor is it "qualified" for *all* offices.

Georgia law states that a party that received a number of votes equal to 1 percent of the number of registered voters in the state is "qualified" for the next election only for statewide office. It may nominate by convention for statewide office without collecting petitions. But if it wishes to run candidates for the U.S. House of Representatives, state legislature, or county office, it must submit separate petitions signed by 5 percent of the number of registered voters. Only if it polls 20 percent for president throughout the entire United States, or 20 percent for governor, may it nominate candidates for district or county office without petitions. Both the Illinois and Georgia laws have been upheld recently in lower federal courts. Thus, Georgia and Illinois make it fairly easy for minor parties to run candidates for statewide office—the type of office they are least likely to win—and make it very difficult to run for lower-level offices. Thus it is not surprising that there have been no minor party victories in these two states in the past fifty years.

Filing Fees Are Low

Since minor parties are almost always short of cash, it is not surprising that a high filing fee inhibits minor parties from running many candidates. Fewer candidates filed means fewer candidates elected. For purposes of this chapter, a "very high" filing fee is one that is equal to at least 1 percent of the salary of the office sought.

Six states have high filing fees for *minor* parties: Florida, Georgia, Montana, Nebraska, Washington, and West Virginia. Seven states have "somewhat high" filing fees (in excess of $200 for some offices but under 1 percent of annual salary): Hawaii, Idaho, Louisiana, Maryland, Nevada, Oklahoma, and Utah. Three states have very high filing fees for major party candidates but not for minor party candidates: California, North Carolina and Texas.

There have been no minor party victories in the six states with very high filing fees nor in the seven states with moderately high fees in the past fifty years. Even relatively low fees discourage minor parties from running candidates. Most of the states in which minor parties have won elections have no filing fees whatsoever.

Conclusion

Table 11.3 summarizes our discussion thus far. As one can readily see, there is a high correlation between minor party victories and the characteristics of state election laws discussed above. The more favorable the state law toward minor parties, the greater the likelihood of minor party success. Only four states have favorable laws in all five respects: Connecticut, New Hampshire, New York, and Vermont. All have had instances of minor party victories since 1945.

Some unfavorable features of state election laws can be more easily overcome by minor parties than others. For example, the lack of fusion is not problematic as other features of the law: in the eighteen states in which minor parties have won elections, thirteen did not permit fusion before 1996. Thus, while legalized fusion is not a necessary condition for minor party success, it appears to help. Even severe ballot access laws are not an absolute barrier to minor party success, as demonstrated

Table 11.3
Minor Party Victories and State Election Laws Since 1945

Minor Party Victories	Federal or State Elections	Local Elections	None
1. Freedom to Nominate:			
Lenient	12.5 percent[1]	31.2 percent	56.3 percent
Restricted	0.0 percent	0.0 percent	100.0 percent
2. Fusion:			
Legal	36.4 percent	36.4 percent	27.2 percent
Illegal	4.7 percent	25.6 percent	69.7 percent
3. Ballot Access:			
Lenient	18.1 percent	45.4 percent	36.3 percent
Moderate	12.0 percent	60.0 percent	48.0 percent
Severe	5.0 percent	0.0 percent	94.4 percent
4. Nomination Regulations:			
Reasonable	12.5 percent	31.3 percent	56.2 percent
Unreasonable	0.0 percent	0.0 percent	100.0 percent
5. Filing Fees:			
Low	14.6 percent	29.2 percent	56.0 percent
High	0.0 percent	0.0 percent	100.0 percent
Very high	0.0 percent	0.0 percent	100.0 percent

1. Rows add to 100 percent.

by a minor party victory in a Tennessee state legislature despite severe ballot access restrictions. However, when states impose high filing fees or make it impossible for a minor party to nominate candidates, minor parties are not able to win elections.

The U.S. Supreme Court has ruled that the First Amendment protects the right of political parties to determine with whom they associate themselves. In *Tashjian v. Republican Party of Connecticut 1986*, the Court even said that it would violate the First Amendment for any state to tell a party that it could not nominate a nonmember. However, many state laws still forbid minor parties, even those that have overcome ballot access laws, to exercise such rights. Perhaps, if the New party wins its lawsuit before the Supreme Court on fusion, lower courts will finally begin to strike down state elections that reduce minor party success.[4]

Notes

1. For the purpose of this chapter, a "minor party" is an organization other than the Democrats or Republicans that runs candidates on a national or statewide basis in at least one state. Parties that are only organized in a single municipality or a single county are excluded, such as municipal parties in Illinois and Connecticut. Also excluded are independent candidates, including presidential candidates, such as George Wallace, who carried states in 1968 under a minor party label. The chapter restricts itself to elections after 1945 because the ballot access laws before then were so different (see Winger 1995).

2. See the Brennan Center for Justice, *Voter Choice '96, a 50-State Report Card on the Presidential Elections* (New York: New York University School of Law) for an attempt to rate state law on ballot access for candidates. Although the Brennan Center's grading system is useful, it is not used here because ballot access for minor parties is much more complicated than for candidates.

3. The term "all elections" includes the November election in all even-numbered years, and if a state elects its governor in an odd year, those odd years are included for that state also.

4. *Timmons et al. v. Twin Cities Area New Party.*

12

Barriers to Minor Party Success and Prospects for Change

Diana Dwyre and Robin Kolodny

The chapters in this volume have given us a sense of how minor parties develop, their current role in the American political system, and how contemporary minor parties plan to address the future. Here we focus on changes that would help minor parties become viable in the United States, and then assess the potential for such changes. We will consider three kinds of barriers to minor party success: cultural biases against minor parties in the electorate; legal obstacles, such as ballot access laws and the structure of elections; and institutional hurdles, such as campaign finance regulations and the lack of media exposure. We conclude that few such changes are likely in the short run, although some modest ones are possible, and they could have significant long-term effects.

Cultural Biases

Scholars have long noted the powerful cultural supports for the two-party system in the United States, which are discussed throughout this book. Thus it is worth asking: Would Americans support minor parties, let alone a multiparty system, even if legal and institutional barriers were removed? Advocates of "multipartyism," such as Kay Lawson (chapter 3) and Richard Winger (chapter 11), answer this question in the affirmative. If minor parties were allowed to compete on an even playing field, they argue, public opinion would eventually become more sympathetic. Other scholars are skeptical of this assertion, including Paul Herrnson (chapter 1) and John Bibby (chapter 4), arguing that the American party system is largely appreciated on its merits, notwithstanding the legal and institutional biases in its favor. There are at least three sources of cultural bias against minor parties. The first element is the way that Americans define democracy. Central to this definition is the notion of majority rule. Specifically, the American electoral system is based on single-member plurality districts with first-past-the-post winners, which discourages candidates who cannot defeat all other opponents from engaging in electoral politics. Thus, to overcome a basic bias in favor of the present system will require Americans to accept alternative definitions of democracy and majority rule, such as proportional representation, multicandidate districts, a parliamentary system of national government, and coalition governments. Indeed, the necessity of such a redefinition lies at the heart of Lawson's argument in favor of a multiparty system.

The second element is more practical: most Americans recognize the entrenchment of the two-party system, so they have a strong incentive to work within it. As a result, the two-party system manages some political discontent reasonably well. The major parties are highly permeable and internally diverse, giving voters and organized interests an opportunity to influence party platforms and the choice of candidates. From this point of view, supporting minor parties is wasted effort and a "wasted vote." Thus, to overcome this practical bias will require Americans to come to view the two-party system as unresponsive to pressing problems or issues. In fact, the success of the system lies at the heart of Bibby's defense of the two-party system, while the possibility of failure is the theme of David Broder's essay that begins the book.

The third element is political: Do minor parties offer plausible alternatives? One of the paradoxes of public support for the two-party system is that the same public appreciates many choices in other aspects of life. However, most Americans do not view minor party platforms or candidates as realistic alternatives to the two major parties; John Green and William Binning (chapter 5) and Christian Collet (chapter 6) suggest why: minor parties tend to combine poor electoral showings with extreme or narrowly focused agendas. As Robert Spitzer shows in his review of the New York "multiparty" system (chapter 7), voters are more likely to support minor parties if they are tied to major party candidates. Of course, minor parties can have a major impact on the two-party system by raising new issues, mobilizing new groups of activists and voters, and putting stress on the major parties, a point well illustrated by Herrnson's review of the American case and Robert Harmel's consideration of the European situation (chapter 2). Thus, to overcome this political bias will require Americans to see minor parties as viable alternatives in their own right.

Legal Obstacles

Legal biases against minor parties in the United States are well known, and this book documents them, especially in Lawson's and Winger's chapters. Here we offer a summary of these problems and possible remedies, including the legal definition of a party, voter registration, ballot access, fusion, and the structure of electoral competition.

The Legal Definition of Party

Perhaps the most perplexing facet of the American political system is the lack of a universal definition of legitimate political actors. There is no one national policy regarding political parties. Instead, the definitions vary by state and by topic. As Winger illustrates, there are over fifty separate definitions of political party for the purposes of ballot access. Each state and the District of Columbia decide how average citizens may engage in party activities through their voter registration laws. They also decide what a political organization must do to attain party status, to nominate candidates, and to retain a position on the ballot. Many of these definitions are hostile to minor parties. The closest thing to a national definition is found in federal campaign finance regulations, such as the rules that stipulate which candidates receive public money in the presidential race and what role parties can play in the financing of congressional campaigns. These national definitions are not particularly favorable to minor parties. Clearly, minor parties would benefit from a more favorable and consistent definition of political party across all governments and all activities.

Voter Registration

The closed nature of voter registration in many states often impedes minor party success. A major problem is the requirement that new parties collect signatures of registered party members in order to appear on the ballot; that is, the signatures of voters registered to their not-yet-existent party. Moreover, giving such support to minor parties often precludes a citizen's participation in other parties. For example, a minor party in West Virginia seeking to acquire ballot position would need to convince voters to sign a petition for their cause, which automatically results in the surrender of their current party registration.

In order to vote in primary elections, many states require voters to declare a party affiliation well in advance of primary election day. While other states have no partisan registration (e.g., Missouri) or have registration on election day (e.g., Illinois), many close registration to new voters or to changes in party affiliation weeks or months before election day. Although the new motor-voter law does make registration easier for citizens by allowing them to register to vote when they apply for a driver's license, it does not change how party registration relates to ballot access or the flexibility citizens have in changing their party affiliation on or before election day. Amending "motor voter" to standardize nonpartisan or open registration across the fifty states would allow minor parties to gain more support from voters who are currently reluctant to give up their opportunity to vote in a major party primary.

Ballot Access

Ballot access laws in the fifty states are often formidable obstacles to minor party success. Simply put, party-nominated candidates have no chance of winning if their names do not appear on the ballot. Also, the U.S. Constitution provides for state governments, not the federal government, to set the time, place, and manner of elections. Some states have structured their conception of guaranteed ballot position to mean that only Democrats and Republicans will get on the ballot automatically each election year. Generally, any party whose candidates received a certain minimum number of votes statewide is spared from having to collect signatures or expend any other effort to remain on the ballot. North Dakota has actually codified the right to ballot position for Democrats and Republicans by name in their ballot access laws, thereby erecting extraordinary barriers for minor parties in that state. On the whole, minor parties must collect signatures, pay fees, and in many states identify individuals who have officially registered as minor party members. These burdens are extremely difficult for minor parties to overcome, as the case of Perot and numerous other candidates reveal. Despite these numerous obstacles, the number of minor party nominees below the presidential level continues to increase, as Collet finds.

In order for minor parties and their candidates to fully participate in American electoral politics, ballot access requirements need to be less daunting. First, the traditional measures of party support used to grant ballot position would have to be relaxed. States would have to require fewer signatures on ballot petitions, not require those who sign ballot petitions to be registered voters of the new or minor party, and reduce or eliminate filing fees. Second, the deadlines for filing ballot petitions should be relatively close to election day to give minor parties more time to organize. Finally, states would have to lower the thresholds currently in place to give political parties automatic ballot position once they have run candidates. Here again, uniformly favorable laws across the states would be desirable. Achieving such a standard would require persuading each state either to adopt less restrictive ballot access laws or to adopt a constitutional amendment to take the power to set the time, place, and manner of elections away from the states and invest it in the federal government. This, of course, would require the assent of thirty-eight state legislatures.

Fusion

Legalized fusion holds some promise for minor parties as well, a point well documented by Spitzer. Fusion allows a candidate to be the nominee of more than one party, thus appearing on multiple party ballot lines. Fusion is legal in just ten states, but only regularly employed in New York. Fusion tickets can make a difference in terms of outcomes (for example, the votes Ronald Reagan received on the Conservative party line helped him win New York in 1980). Fusion makes it easier for minor parties to realize some success because fusion tickets allow citizens to vote for a minor party without feeling they have wasted their vote.

The U.S. Supreme Court recently ruled on the legality of banning fusion in *Timmons et al. v. Twin Cities Area New Party* (1997). The defendant in the case, the New Party, claimed that a Minnesota law banning fusion tickets was a violation of the party's First Amendment right of free association. The ban was declared unconstitutional by a U.S. appeals court and the state of Minnesota appealed to the Supreme Court. Minnesota's assistant solicitor general argued that the state forbids fusion to prevent voter confusion and to guard against ballot manipulation. The high court overturned the appeals court decision, finding that Minnesota's law against fusion was permissible, though they did not rule fusion itself unconstitutional. The ruling confirmed the right of states to regulate access to the ballot in ways that may discourage minor party participation.

The Electoral System

Scholars have long known that the nature of the American practice of single-member plurality elections discourages minor parties. By having only one winner in each of several hundred districts, minor parties have to garner a significant amount of support to make even a small dent in the composition of the national legislature. Perhaps more important, only one view (that of the plurality winner) gets represented in the government, often denying a majority (who did not support the winner) its say. As Harmel and Lawson argue, the multiparty systems in Europe have very different election laws, usually with some form of proportional representation. Not surprisingly, some minor parties in the U.S. have endorsed proportional representation. A good example is the Green party (chapter 10), whose interest derives in part from the party's origins in European Green parties.

The anti-minor party effects of single-member plurality elections are compounded by the Electoral College. Presidents are not elected by popular vote, but are chosen by the Electoral College. Electoral College members are selected in each state based on the state's popular vote. The method of choosing electors is left up the state. Currently, forty-eight states and the District of Columbia have adopted what are essentially single-member plurality elections: winner-take-all on the basis of a plurality of the vote. Maine and Nebraska have different systems. Maine, for example, has a mixed apportionment system in which the winner of each congressional district wins that district's elector and the winner of the statewide vote wins the two "senatorial" electors. However, election results in Maine have paralleled the winner-take-all system. This system discourages minor parties from seeking the presidency because they must defeat all others in a state to obtain any electoral votes. Major party candidate defeats have occurred when minor party or independent candidates have run strong regional campaigns, such as Strom Thurmond in 1948 and George Wallace in 1968. Had they won enough electoral votes to deny one major party candidate a majority of the Electoral College votes, their efforts could have forced the election into the House of Representatives. However, if a minor party has broad-based national support, even an impressive showing at the polls may produce no electors, such as with Ross Perot in 1992 and 1996.

To increase minor party influence, states could abandon the winner-take-all method of apportioning electoral votes in favor of some form of proportional representation. Even following the Maine system of apportioning electors by congressional district would allow minor party candidates a greater chance of success. If minor parties were to regularly win electors and the majority requirement to elect the president were maintained, they could influence the choice of president as part of a coalition, or send the election into the House of Representatives. In any event, almost any move away from single-member plurality elections to proportional representation would benefit minor parties.

Institutional Hurdles

In addition to legal obstacles, minor parties face severe hurdles in acquiring the resources and exposure to be effective in politics. Some of these hurdles are based in statutes, such as federal campaign finance laws, and others are based in custom, such as access to the media. We will consider two examples of these problems at the national level; there are no doubt countless more problems at the state and local levels.

Campaign Finance

The Federal Election Campaign Act (FECA) is a significant impediment to minor party success at the presidential level. First, the FECA encourages serious presidential candidates to pursue major party nominations through its system of matching funds in primaries and caucuses. Second, the FECA provides significant funding for the major party national nominating conventions and full public funding for major party candidates' general election campaigns (payable to those campaigns as soon as the nomination is made official). For these purposes, the FECA defines a major party as a political party whose candidate for the office of president in the preceding presidential election received, as a candidate of such party, 25 percent or more of the total number of popular votes received by all candidates for president.

Third, the FECA treats minor parties differently from major parties. A minor party is defined as one whose candidate for president received between 5 and 25 percent of the presidential vote. Minor parties can receive some public financing. New minor parties can be reimbursed for individual contributions raised under FECA rules after the election if they receive 5 percent or more of the vote. In subsequent elections, minor parties and their presidential candidates can receive advance payments in proportion to the vote they received in the previous election (as Perot did in 1996). The FECA gives federal matching funds to any minor (or major) party candidate who raised at least $5,000 in amounts of $250 or less in twenty states. Minor parties are entitled to partial funding for their national nominating conventions and the general election based on their performance in the previous presidential election compared to that of the major parties. Minor party fund-raising is also subject to the same contribution limits as major parties, which can be a serious burden because minor parties usually have a smaller base of contributors from which to raise funds. After all, Perot's personal funds in 1992 and 1996 made the Reform party possible. To enjoy the benefits of such a patron, minor parties must operate outside of the FECA.

Unlike most of the legal obstacles discussed above, the FECA does provide some benefits to minor parties, but not on par with the major parties. A more level playing field could be established by expanding the definition of a minor party. For example, the standard could be lowered to 2.5 percent of either the presidential vote or the aggregate congressional vote in a previous election (many European countries have thresholds of 1 percent or less). New parties could receive matching funds based on the number of congressional candidates they field, the number of contributors, or their strength in opinion polls. Along these lines, larger subsidies for party conventions and nomination efforts could be provided.

Finally, minor parties should not have to meet the demanding current requirements to attain national committee status. Recently, the Federal Election Commission (FEC) declared the organization designated by the Green party as its national committee to be "insufficiently active" to qualify as such. The definition of "national committee" is important because it determines how much money a party can raise from various sources. The FEC's ruling forces the Green party to raise money in much smaller increments than the major parties, clearly putting the Greens at a disadvantage.

Media Exposure

A significant deterrent to minor party success is the lack of media attention. This problem applies to both "earned" and "paid" media. On the first count, journalists are inclined to report elections as events and therefore give more attention to the horse-race aspects of campaigns (e.g., poll results, candidate gaffes, negative ads) than to policy issues. This bias leads to heavier news coverage of well-established candidates, to the detriment of minor parties, and extends to media events, such as candidate debates and national conventions. Minor party candidates are routinely excluded from the debates, even when they are prominent (such as Perot in 1996), while their conventions are rarely covered at all. On the second count, the costs of the mass media are prohibitive for most minor party candidates and media outlets have been known to refuse to sell time even to well-heeled parties (which also happened to Perot in 1996).

The major criterion for most forms of media exposure is "electability," which minor parties are hard-pressed to demonstrate. Of course, the electability standard can become a self-fulfilling prophecy, with lack of attention dooming minor parties to a poor finish. Several kinds of reforms might help minor parties gain exposure and thus become newsworthy. One idea would be to provide political parties and their candidates, including minor parties, with free broadcast time through communications vouchers and/or an "equal time" provision. Another idea would be to expand the number of party candidates normally included in the nationally televised presidential debates. Also, broadcasters could be required to provide coverage to all candidates on the ballot as a condition of holding a broadcast license, a sort of "public service programming" extended to political candidates. As with campaign finance, almost any change in this area would help minor parties.

Prospects for Change

Having identified a number of changes that would help make minor parties more successful, we now turn to the likelihood that they will be adopted in the near future. One can easily imagine three sources of change: pressure from within the major parties, the court system, and the ballot box. Each of these sources of change is likely to have the most effect, respectively, on the cultural biases, legal obstacles, and institutional hurdles that minor parties face. Given the magnitude of the challenge, we doubt that major changes will occur soon, but some modest alterations are possible, and they could have long-term repercussions.

Since the major parties control all governmental institutions, significant reforms are unlikely. Indeed, many of the barriers that minor parties face were deliberately erected by the major parties, and more could be created, particularly if minor parties became a threat. Thus, major changes, such as the substitution of proportional representation instead of single-member plurality elections, mandating that all states use proportional representation to allocate Electoral College votes, or the adoption of uniform ballot access laws, are very unlikely in the short run.

However, one should not completely count out the major parties as a source of change. For one thing, they have great opportunities for failure. In fact, it is major party failure that prompts most minor party activity in the first place. The more dramatic the failure, the larger the potential changes. The most significant impact of major party failure is the erosion of cultural biases in favor of the two-party system. There is nothing quite like poor government to undermine the philosophical, practical, and political supports of the party system among the citizenry. Elected officials, interest group leaders, journalists, pundits, and scholars can all be effective critics of the party system. Although many political elites are committed firmly to the present arrangements, others have a passion for reform.

Another potential source of change is the court system. Minor parties are frequently in court arguing that they are denied their political rights. To the extent that such challenges are successful at the state and federal levels, the legal obstacles to minor parties can be removed or mitigated. State law is particularly vulnerable to court challenges. Suits over ballot access were successful in the past two decades to the benefit of minor parties. But in *Timmons et al. v. Twin Cities Area New Party* (1997), the Supreme Court dealt minor parties a significant blow by upholding Minnesota's ban against fusion by minor parties with major party candidates. Though states like New York may still have fusion tickets, the majority's rationale for their decision sets a foreboding precedent. Chief Justice William Rehnquist wrote that ". . . States may, and inevitably must, enact reasonable regulations of parties, elections, and ballots to reduce election- and campaign-related disorder." The court's finding that minor party rights may mean "disorder" in our politics will certainly impede efforts for minor party ballot access in the future. Indeed, in a dissenting opinion in this case, Justice John Paul Stevens bluntly acknowledged that the real reason for the decision has to do with a disdain for minor parties rather than a genuine concern for order: "The fact that the law was both intended to disadvantage minor parties and has had that effect . . . should weigh against, rather than in favor of its constitutionality."

A final source of change is the minor parties themselves and their impact at the ballot box. Any gains minor parties make in elections can help change the system in their favor by pushing the present limits of political institutions. This process is also likely to be slow, eroding hurdles in campaign finance and media exposure, which, in turn, can help minor parties compete in subsequent elections. Although minor parties may never gain power by their efforts alone, it is hard to see how the system could become more favorable to them without persistent activity. On the one hand, minor party activity can put pressure on the major parties, and on the other hand, minor parties must be poised to take advantage of failures by the major parties or a legal breakthrough if their status is to improve dramatically. The consequence of discouraging minor party participation is the encouragement of independent candidates, who generally have an easier time getting on the ballot than minor party candidates. Thus the idea of conducting politics through parties becomes compromised, a result few observers seem to desire.

In summary, few of these changes are likely to be enacted in the short run. Yet there is the possibility that some modest changes will materialize and their long-term cumulative effects could be significant. The question we cannot yet answer is this: Will such changes make minor parties more effective participants in the American political system, or will the system itself change, producing multiparty politics in America?

References

Abramson, Paul R., John H. Aldrich, Phil Paolino, and David W. Rohde. 1995. "Third-Party and Independent Candidates: Wallace, Anderson, and Perot." *Political Science Quarterly* 110, (Fall): 349–68.

Affigne, Anthony DeSales. 1995. "Transforming the Political Landscape: The Transformation of the Individual, 'Fractal Politics,' and Emerging Alliances Among Green and Progressive Parties in the United States." Paper presented at the Annual Meeting of the American Political Science Association, Chicago.

Aldrich, John H., and Richard G. Niemi. 1996. "The Sixth Party System: Electoral Change, 1952–1992," in Stephen C. Craig, ed. *Broken Contract? Changing Relationships Between Americans and Their Government.* Boulder, Colo.: Westview Press.

Alexander, Herbert E., and Anthony Corrado. 1995. *Financing the 1992 Election.* Armonk, N.Y.: Sharpe.

Arnold, Jacqualine. 1995. "Party Lines Tug Executive Candidate." *Syracuse Post-Standard* (June 16), C3.

Associated Press. 1996. "Perot Launches Reform Party Presidential Campaign." (August 25).

Ayres, R. Drummond. 1996. "The Spoilers Take Their Marks." *New York Times* (August 25), WR2.

Babbington, Charles. 1996. "Reform Party Falters in Washington Area as Perot Loses Luster with Backers." *Washington Post* (August 9).

Baker, Donald P. 1996a. "Perot Gets Reform Party Nod." *Washington Post* (August 18).

———. 1996b. "Reform Party Candidates Grumble: Where's Ross Perot." *Washington Post* (November 3).

Ballot Access News. 1996. 12(7), September 9.

———. 1997. "1996 'Official' Presidential Vote." 12(11): January 12.

Balz, Dan. 1994. "Candidates Wage the War of Independents." *Washington Post National Weekly Edition* 11 (September 19–25): 13–14.

Barnes, James A. 1993. "Still on the Trail." *National Journal* (April 10).

Bauder, David. 1993. "Supporters of Gay Rights Criticize Fear of Conservatives." *Cortland Standard* (June 3), 11.

Beck, Paul Allen. 1997. *Party Politics in America,* 8th ed. New York: Longman.

Bibby, John F. 1987. *Politics, Parties, and Elections in America.* Chicago: Nelson-Hall.

Bielski, Vince. 1996. "What's Your Preference?" *San Francisco Weekly.* (October 23), 10.

Biersack, Robert. 1994. "Hard Facts and Soft Money: State Party Finance in the 1992 Federal Elections," in John C. Green and Daniel M. Shea, eds. *The*

State of the Parties: The Changing Role of Contemporary American Parties. Lanham, Md.: Rowman & Littlefield.

Black, Gordon S. 1972. "A Theory of Political Ambition: Career Choices and the Role of Structural Incentives." *American Political Science Review* 66 (March): 144–159.

Bleifuss, Joel. 1995. "Voting Matters." *In These Times* (November 27): 13.

Bonnar, Raymond. 1996. "Bosnia Gears up for Election, with 25,000 Candidates." *New York Times* (July 21): 8.

Brams, Steven J. 1978. *The Presidential Election Game.* New Haven: Yale University Press.

Broder, David S. 1970. *The Party's Over: The Failure of Politics in America.* New York: Harper & Row.

———. 1996. "The Party's Over: By 2000, the GOP or the Democrats Could Fade in Favor for a Third Party." *Washington Post* (August 11), C1, C4.

Brogan, Dennis W. 1954. *Politics in America.* New York: Harper.

Bruni, Frank. 1996. "Reform Party Has Made a New Alliance." *Akron Beacon Journal.* (September 1), G1.

Burnham, Walter Dean. 1970. *Critical Elections and the Mainsprings of American Politics* New York: Norton.

Canfield, James Lewis. 1984. *A Case of Third Party Activism.* Lanham Md.: University Press of America.

Canon, David T. 1990. *Actors, Athletes and Astronauts.* Chicago: University of Chicago Press.

———. 1993. "Sacrificial Lambs or Strategic Politicians? Political Amateurs in U.S. House Elections." *American Journal of Political Science* 37 (November): 1119–41.

Carroll, Maurice. 1982a. "State Democrats Attack Cross-Endorsement Policy." *New York Times* (January 29), B-2.

———. 1982b. "Minor Party Once Again Has a Major Effect on Politics." *New York Times* (March 14), E-7.

Ceaser, James, and Andrew Busch. 1993. *Upside Down and Inside Out: The 1992 Elections and American Politics.* Lanham, Md.: Rowman & Littlefield.

Clarke, Peter, and Susan Evans. 1983. *Covering Campaigns: Journalism in Congressional Elections.* Stanford: Stanford University Press.

Collet, Christian. 1996. "Poll Trends: Third Parties and the Two Party System." *Public Opinion Quarterly* 60 (Fall): 587–613.

Corrado, Anthony. 1997. "Financing the 1996 Elections," in Gerald M. Pomper, ed. *The Election of 1996.* Chatham, NJ: Chatham House.

Crotty, William. 1984. *American Parties in Decline.* Boston: Little, Brown.

Downs, Anthony. 1957. *An Economic Theory of Democracy.* New York: HarperCollins.

Duverger, Maurice. 1954. *Political Parties: Their Organization and Activity in the Modern State*, trans. Barbara and Robert North, 2nd ed. New York: Wiley.

———. 1963. *Political Parties.* New York: Wiley.

The Economist. 1993. "A Wide Choice of Ways to Choose 327" (May 1): 20.

Elden, James M., and David R. Schweitzer. 1971. "New Third Party Radicalism: The Case of the California Peace and Freedom Party." *Western Political Quarterly* 24: 761–74.

Eldersveld, Samuel J. 1982. *Political Parties in American Society.* New York: Basic Books.

Epstein, Leon D. 1980. *Political Parties in Western Democracies.* New Brunswick, N.J.: Transaction.

———. 1986. *Political Parties in the American Mold.* Madison: University of Wisconsin Press.

Fischer, John. 1948. "Unwritten Rules of American Politics." *Harper's* 197 (November), 27–36.

Fisher, Ian. 1994. "Minor Parties File Petitions for Pataki and Rosenbaum." *New York Times* (August 24), B4.

Fisher, Marc. 1996. "The Unconventional Party." *Washington Post* (August 12).

Flanagan, Scott C. 1987. "Value Change in Industrial Societies." *American Political Science Review* 81: 1303–19.

Flood, Emmet T., and William G. Mayer. 1996. "Third-Party and Independent Candidates," in William G. Mayer, ed., *In Pursuit of the White House: How We Choose Our Presidential Nominees.* Chatham, N.J.: Chatham House.

Freie, John F. 1982. "Minor Parties in Realigning Eras." *American Politics Quarterly* 10: 42–63.

Ganz, Marshall. 1994. "Voters in the Crosshairs: Elections and Voter Turnout." *American Prospect* (Winter): 4–10.

Gillespie, J. David. 1993. *Politics at the Periphery: Third Parties in Two-Party America.* Columbia: University of South Carolina Press.

Gimpel, James. 1996. *National Elections and the Autonomy of American State Elections.* Pittsburgh: University of Pittsburgh Press.

Goodwyn, Lawrence. 1978. *The Populist Movement.* New York: Cambridge University Press.

Graber, Doris A. 1993. *Mass Media in American Politics.* Washington, D.C.: Congressional Quarterly Press.

Green, John C., and James L. Guth. 1994. "Controlling the Mischief of Factions: Party Support and Coalition Building Among Party Activists," in John C. Green, ed., *Politics, Professionalism and Power.* Lanham, Md.: University Press of America.

Green Party of California. 1996. *Green Party of California Policy Directions.* San Francisco: Green Leaf.

Greenberg, Stanley B. 1995. *Middle Class Dreams: The Politics and Power of the New American Majority.* New Haven: Yale University Press.

Greenblatt, Alan. 1996. "Reform Party's Chief Rivals: David and Goliath?" *Congressional Quarterly Weekly Report* (July 27).

Greenhouse, Linda. 1996. "Law Barring Multiparty Ballot Listing of a Single Candidate is Challenged." *New York Times* (May 29), A14.

Greenhouse, Linda. 1996b. "Supreme Court Debates State Bans on Multiparty Candidates." *New York Times* (December 5), A12.

Greenstein, Fred I. 1970. *The American Party System and the American People,* 2nd ed. Englewood Cliffs, N.J.: Prentice-Hall.

Guth, James L., and John C. Green. 1996. "Balance Wheels: Minor Party Activists in the Two-Party System," in *The State of the Parties: The Changing Role of Contemporary American Parties*, 2nd ed. John C. Green and Daniel M. Shea, eds. Lanham, Md.: Rowman & Littlefield.

Hall, Mimi. 1996a. "Former Perot Backers Facing Off with Headquarters." *USA Today* (July 10).

———. 1996b. "USA Passion for Perot Wanes." *USA Today* (August 12).

———. 1996c. "Perot Asks Supporters to Match Federal Campaign Funds." *USA Today* (August 18).

———. 1996d. "Perot Party's Legacy Could Be Its Effort." *USA Today* (November 5).

———. 1996e. "Third Party Efforts Persist Despite Limited Success." *USA Today* (November 6).

Hannagan, Charley. 1989. "Small Conservative Party Still Powerful in Cayuga County." *Syracuse Post-Standard* (June 6), C3.

Harmel, Robert, and John D. Robertson. 1985. "Formation and Success of New Parties: A Cross-National Analysis." *International Political Science Review* 6: 513–19.

Harmel, Robert, and Lars Svåsand. 1990. "The Impacts of New Political Parties: The Cases of the Danish and Norwegian Progress Parties." Paper presented at the Annual Meeting of the American Political Science Association, San Francisco.

———. 1997. "The Influence of New Parties on Old Parties' Platforms: The Cases of the Progress Parties and Conservative Parties of Denmark and Norway." *Party Politics*. Vol. 3, No. 3 (July), 315–40.

Hazlett, Joseph M., II. 1992. *The Libertarian Party and Other Minor Political Parties in the United States*. Jefferson, N.C.: McFarland.

Herring, Pendleton. 1940. *The Politics of Democracy*. New York: Rinehart.

Herrnson, Paul S. 1988. *Party Campaigning in the 1980s*. Cambridge: Harvard University Press.

———. 1995. *Congressional Elections: Campaigning at Home and in Washington*. Washington, D.C.: Congressional Quarterly Press.

Hill, Steven, and Richard DeLeon. 1996. "Will S.F. Give Voters a Choice?" *San Francisco Chronicle* (July 11).

Hoffman, Milton. 1982. "Major Parties Might Lose Top Ballot Positions." *Ithaca Journal* (August 26), 10.

Huckshorn, Robert J., and Robert C. Spencer. 1971. *The Politics of Defeat: Campaigning for Congress*. Amherst: University of Massachusetts Press.

Inglehart, Ronald. 1987. "Value Change in Industrial Societies." *American Political Science Review* 81 (December): 1289–1303.

———. 1990. *Culture Shift in Advanced Industrial Democracies*. Princeton: Princeton University Press.

Jacobson, Gary C., and Samuel Kernell. 1983. *Strategy and Choice in Congressional Elections,* 2nd ed. New Haven: Yale University Press.

Jost, Kenneth. 1995. "Third-Party Prospects." *CQ Researcher*. Washington, D.C.: Congressional Quarterly Press.

Kaid, Lynda Lee, and Christina Holtz-Bacha, eds. 1995. *Political Advertising in*

Western Democracies: Parties and Candidates on Television. Thousand Oaks, Calif.: Sage.

Karen, Robert. 1975. "The Politics of Pressure." *The Nation* (September 20): 236–37.

Keefe, William J. 1994. *Political Parties and Public Policy in America.* Washington, D.C.: Congressional Quarterly Press.

Keith, Bruce E., David B. Magleby, Candice J. Nelson, Elizabeth Orr, Mark C. Westlye, and Raymond E. Wolfinger. 1992. *The Myth of the Independent Voter.* Berkeley: University of California Press.

Kendall, Willmoore, and Austin Ranney. 1956. *Democracy and the American Party System.* New York: Harcourt, Brace.

Key, V. O., Jr. 1964. *Politics, Parties, and Pressure Groups in America,* 5th ed. New York: Crowell.

Kitschelt, Herbert. 1990. "New Social Movements and the Decline of Party Organization," in Russell J. Dalton and Manfred Kuechler eds. *Challenging the Political Order.* New York: Oxford University Press.

Kriss, Erik. 1995. "State GOP Controls Third Party." *Syracuse Herald American* (September 17), G7.

Lijphart, Arend. 1977. *Democracy in Plural Society: A Comparative Exploration.* New Haven: Yale University Press.

———. 1984. *Democracies: Patterns of Majoritarian and Consensus Government in Twenty-One Countries.* New Haven: Yale University Press.

———. 1994. *Electoral Systems and Party Systems: A Study of Twenty-Seven Democracies 1945–1990.* Oxford: Oxford University Press.

Lind, Michael. 1992. "A Radical Plan to Change American Politics," *Atlantic Monthly* (August): 78–81.

Lipset, Seymour Martin, and Stein Rokkan. 1967. *Party Systems and Voter Alignments: Cross-National Perspectives.* New York: Free Press.

Lowi, Theodore J. 1996a. "A Ticket to Democracy," *New York Times* (December 28), 21.

———. 1996b. "Toward a Responsible Three-Party System: Prospects and Obstacles," in John C. Green and Daniel M. Shea, eds. *The State of the Parties: The Changing Role of Contemporary American Parties,* 2nd ed. Lanham, Md.: Rowman & Littlefield.

———. 1996c. "Hot Fusion? Labor, Independent Politics, and Post–1996 Organizing," *New Party News* 3 (Fall): 1, 10.

Lynn, Frank. 1982. "Conservatives and a Political Gamble in New York." *New York Times* (January 26), B-7.

———. 1986. "Right to Life Candidate Tries to Make Abortion an Issue." *New York Times* (September 21), B-3.

Mair, Peter. 1991. "The Electoral Universe of Small Parties in Postwar Western Europe," in Ferdinand Müller-Rommel and Geoffrey Pridham, eds., *Small Parties in Western Europe: Comparative and National Perspectives.* London and Newbury Park, Calif.: Sage.

Maisel, Louis Sandy. 1982. *From Obscurity to Oblivion.* Knoxville: University of Tennessee Press.

————, ed. 1991. "Fusion Party in New York City," *Political Parties and Elections in the United States*, 2 vols. New York: Garland, I: 417.

Margolis, Michael, and John C. Green. 1995. "Political Parties in Ohio," in Carl Lieberman, ed. *Government, Politics and Public Policy in Ohio*. Akron: Midwest Press.

Mazmanian, David. 1974. *Third Parties in Presidential Elections*. Washington, D.C.: Brookings Institution.

Miller, Karin. 1996. "Reform Party Conference Factious." *Associated Press* (January 26).

Mitchell, Alison. 1993. "Liberals and Republicans Scrambling for Giuliani Jobs." *New York Times* (December 20), B1.

Moore, David W. 1996. "The Party Isn't Over." *The Public Perspective* 7: 1–3.

Moscow, Warren. 1948. *Politics in the Empire State*. New York: Knopf.

Müller-Rommel, Ferdinand, ed. 1989. *New Politics in Western Europe: The Rise and the Success of Green Parties and Alternative Lists*. Boulder, Colo.: Westview.

————. 1990. "New Political Movements and 'New Politics' Parties in Western Europe," in Russell J. Dalton and Manfred Kuechler, eds. *Challenging the Political Order*. New York: Oxford.

Nassmacher, Karl-Heinz. 1993. "Comparing Party and Campaign Finance in Western Democracies." *Campaign and Party Finance in North America and Western Europe*. Boulder, Colo.: Westview Press.

The Nation. [*1996.*] "Equalizing the Vote" (October 14): 6.

Nelson, Michael. 1997. "The Election: Turbulence and Tranquility in Contemporary American Politics," in Michael Nelson, ed., *The Elections of 1996*. Washington, D.C.: Congressional Quarterly Press.

Neumeister, Lawrence. 1986. "Dillon: Victory Is Not Main Issue." *Cortland Standard* (October 27), 4.

Nolan, Maureen. 1995. "State's Party Policy Complicates Elections." *Syracuse Post-Standard* (November 6), C3.

Oreskes, Michael. 1985. "Election Law Battles a Tradition in New York." *New York Times* (August 25), B4.

Partin, Randall W., Lori M. Weber, Ronald B. Rapoport, and Walter J. Stone. 1994. "Sources of Activism in the 1992 Perot Campaign," in John C. Green and Daniel M. Shea, eds. *The State of the Parties: The Changing Role of Contemporary American Parties*. Lanham, Md.: Rowman & Littlefield.

————. 1996. "Perot Activists in 1992 and 1994: Sources of Activism," in John C. Green and Daniel M. Shea, eds. *The State of the Parties: The Changing Role of Contemporary American Parties,* 2nd ed. Lanham, Md.: Rowman & Littlefield.

Pinchot, Amos R. E. 1958. *History of the Progressive Party 1912–1916*. New York: New York University Press.

Polsby, Nelson W., and Aaron Wildavsky. 1996. *Presidential Elections: Strategies and Structures in American Politics*, 9th ed. Chatham, N.J.: Chatham House.

Pomper, Gerald M. 1997. "The Presidential Election," in Gerald M. Pomper, ed. *The Election of 1996*. Chatham, N.J.: Chatham House.

Purdum, Todd S. 1993. "Mayoral Race May Turn on Slivers of Liberal Vote." *New York Times* (August 12), 1.

Putnam, Robert D. 1976. *The Comparative Study of Political Elites.* Englewood Cliffs, N.J.: Prentice-Hall.

Ranney, Austin. 1975. *Curing the Mischiefs of Faction.* Berkeley: University of California Press.

Ranney, Austin, and Willmoore Kendall. 1956. *Democracy and the American Party System.* New York: Harcourt and Brace.

Reform Party. 1996a. "Reform Party and NYS Independence Party Join Forces." Press Release (June 25).

————. 1996b. "For Our Children and Grandchildren: A History of the Reform Party." Press Release (September).

Riker, William H. 1982. "The Two-Party System and Duverger's Law: An Essay on the History of Political Science." *American Political Science Review* 76: 753–64.

Roberts, Sam. 1989. "Tiny Liberal Party Set to Wag Some Big Dogs." *New York Times* (March 13), B1.

Rochon, Thomas R. 1985. "Mobilizers and Challengers: Toward a Theory of New Party Success." *International Political Science Review* 6: 419–40.

Rohde, David W. 1979. "Risk-Bearing and Progressive Ambition: The Case of Members of the United States House of Representatives." *American Journal of Political Science* 23 (February): 1–26.

Rose, Richard. 1984. *Do Parties Make a Difference?* Chatham, N.J.: Chatham House.

Rosenstone, Steven J., Roy L. Behr, and Edward H. Lazarus. 1984. *Third Parties in America: Citizen Response to Major Party Failure.* Princeton: Princeton University Press.

————. 1996. *Third Parties in America: Citizen Response to Major Party Failure,* rev. ed. Princeton: Princeton University Press.

Rule, Wilma, Steven Hill, and Sandy Fernandes. 1996. "Voting for a Change." *Ms.* (September/October): 26.

Sack, Kevin. 1994. "A Liberal's Patronage Dividend." *New York Times* (February 15), B3.

Salit, Jacqueline. 1996. "The Patriot Party and the Reform Party." *Patriot Party Newsletter* (May).

Sartori, Giovanni. 1976. *Parties and Party Systems.* Cambridge: Cambridge University Press.

Scarrow, Howard. 1983. *Parties, Elections, and Representation in the State of New York.* New York: New York University Press, 1983.

————. 1986. "Duverger's Law, Fusion, and the Decline of American 'Third' Parties." *Western Political Quarterly* 39: 634–47.

Schattschneider, E. E. 1942. *Party Government.* New York: Holt, Rinehart and Winston.

Schmidt, Karl M. 1960. *Henry A. Wallace: Quixotic Crusade.* Syracuse: Syracuse University Press.

Schmidt, William E. 1992. "Eighty Parties Vie for Czechoslovaks' Votes." *International Herald Tribune* (June 2): 7.

Schoenberger, Robert A. 1968. "Conservatism, Personality and Political Extremism." *American Political Science Review* 62: 869.

Shan, Chao-Chi. 1991. "The Decline of Electoral Competition in New York State Senate Elections, 1950–1988." Ph.D. dissertation, Syracuse University.

Smallwood, Frank, 1983. *The Other Candidates: Third Parties in Presidential Elections*. Hanover, Conn.: Yale University Press.

Smith, Gordon. 1991. "In Search of Small Parties: Problems of Definition, Classification and Significance," in Ferdinand Müller-Rommel and Geoffrey Pridham, eds. *Small Parties in Western Europe*. London: Sage.

Sorauf, Frank J. 1980. "Political Parties and Political Action Committees: Two Life Cycles." *Arizona Law Review* 22: 445–64.

Spitzer, Robert J. 1984. "A Political Party Is Born: Single-Issue Advocacy and the New York State Election Law." *National Civic Review* (July/August): 323–24.

———. 1987. *The Right to Life Movement and Third Party Politics*. Westport, Conn.: Greenwood Press.

Sundquist, James L. 1973. *The Dynamics of the Two-Party System*. Washington, D.C.: Brookings Institution.

———. 1983. *The Dynamics of the Two-Party System,* rev. ed.. Washington, D.C.: Brookings Institution.

Syracuse Post-Standard. 1995. "New York Party to Work for Perot" (September 27), A8.

Washington Post. 1995. November 6, A11.

———. 1996. "There's the Ticket . . . A Selection of Running Mates for Ross Perot." September 7.

Wilson, Basil. 1993. "Fifty Years of Party Politics in Jamaica." *Everybody's* (July): 15–18.

Winger, Richard. 1995. "How Ballot Access Laws Affect the U.S. Party System." *American Review of Politics* 16: 321–50.

Yarrow, Andrew L. 1992. "Third Party Celebrates Its Second Year." *New York Times* (July 27), B5.

Zimmerman, Joseph F. 1981. *The Government and Politics of New York State*. New York: New York University Press.

———. 1994. "Alternative Voting Systems for Representative Democracy." *P.S.: Political Science and Politics* 27:4 (December): 674–77.

Index

References followed by "n" indicate endnotes; references followed by "f", "t", or "n" indicate figures, tables, or footnotes, respectively.

110, 112*t*; reasons for leaving major parties, 110–12, 113*t*; social characteristics, 110, 111*t*

New Mexico: ballot access laws, 166; Green movement, 155–56; nomination laws, 162–63; support for Perot, 94*t*

new parties, 43–57, 57n8; categories of, 46–47; challenging, 46; cross-national comparison, 48–49; electoral success, 44–46, 45*t*, 47, 52; formation of, 52; frequency of, 47, 47*t*; government participation, 44–46; impacts on old parties' issue positions, 49–52; on issues, 46–47; mobilizing, 46; personality-based, 56; promotion of, 54. *See also* minor parties; *specific parties*

New party, 68; *Timmons et al. v. Twin Cities Area New Party*, 16, 68, 137n7, 164, 177, 182

new politics parties, 108, 121n3

New Progressive party, 33

new right, 14–15, 121n3. *See also* Libertarian party

New York City: mayoral elections, 130–31, 133–35; minor party victories, 159–60, 161*t*

New Yorker, 70

New York State, 125–37; ballot access laws, 136n4, 166; cross-endorsements or fusion tickets, 15, 36–37, 68, 125, 128–31, 137n6, 137n9, 164, 177, 182; election laws, 129–32, 137n5, 169; gubernatorial elections, 133–35; history and political culture, 126–28; minor parties, 126–28, 133–35, 136n1, 137n8; minor party victories, 159–60, 160*t*–161*t*; small party candidates, 122n6; support for Perot, 94*t*; third parties, 129–30

New York Times, 70, 135, 137n10

New Zealand, 66–67

NFIB. *See* National Federation of Independent Business

nominations: minor party procedures, 162–63, 167–69; participatory, 25. *See also* fusion tickets

nonpartisanship, 71n6

North Carolina: ballot access laws, 166; filing fees, 169; Green movement, 155; support for Perot, 94*t*

North Dakota: ballot access laws, 166, 176; fusion tickets, 164; support for Perot, 94*t*

Norway: Conservative party, 50–52, 58n9; Progress party, 49–56, 58n9

NRA, 99, 99*t*

Nunn, Sam, 7, 9

O'Connor, Frank, 131

Ohio: ballot access laws, 166; support for Perot, 93, 94*t*

Ohio Reform party: activists, 93–101; issues and ideology, 99–101, 100*t*; motivations, goals, activity, 96–97, 97*t*; partisanship, 93–95, 95*t*; proximity to leaders and groups, 98–99, 99*t*

Oklahoma: ballot access laws, 166; filing fees, 169; minor party nominees, 162; support for Perot, 94*t*

old left parties, 14, 123*t*

old left party candidates: partisanship and loyalty of, 116–18, 117*t*; political background, experience and activity, 114, 115*t*; previous party affiliation, 110, 112*t*; reasons for leaving major parties, 110–12, 113*t*; social characteristics, 110, 111*t*

old right parties, 14, 124*t*

old right party candidates: partisanship and loyalty of, 116–18, 117*t*; political background, experience and activity, 114, 115*t*; previous party affiliation, 110, 112*t*; reasons for leaving major parties, 110–12, 113*t*; social characteristics, 110, 111*t*

Oregon: ballot access laws, 166; support for Perot, 94*t*

O'Rourke, Andrew, 127

other issue parties, 46–47, 47*t*

Ottinger, Richard, 131

Pacific party, 17n1

PACs. *See* political action committees

About the Editors and Contributors

John F. Bibby is professor of political science at the University of Wisconsin-Milwaukee, specializing in the study of American political parties. He is the author of *Politics, Parties, and Elections in America* and a coauthor of *Party Organizations in American Politics*.

William C. Binning is professor and chair of political science at Youngstown State University. His most recent writing has been on Ohio politics.

David S. Broder is a syndicated columnist for *The Washington Post* and has written extensively on national politics. His best known book is *The Party's Over* (1967).

Christian Collet is a Ph.D. candidate in the Department of Politics and Society at University of California, Irvine.

Diana Dwyre is assistant professor of political science at the California State University, Chico. Her research interests include party organizations, elections, and Congress, and she is the 1998 American Political Science Association Steiger Congressional Fellow.

John C. Green is professor of political science and director of the Ray C. Bliss Institute of Applied Politics at the University of Akron. His most recent publication is the edited volume *The State of the Parties* (1996).

Robert Harmel is professor of political science at Texas A & M University. He has written extensively on comparative political parties. His most recent research has been on the topics of new political parties and party changes.

Paul S. Herrnson is professor of government and politics at the University of Maryland at College Park. His most recent books are *Congressional Elections: Campaigning at Home and in Washington* (1995) and *The Interest Group Connection: Electioneering, Lobbying and Policymaking in Washington* (1997), coedited with Ron Shaiko and Clyde Wilcox.

Greg Jan is a founding member of the Green party of California and has been active since 1985. From 1986-1988, he served on the Governing Council of National Green Party, and in 1996 he chaired the Committee to Draft Ralph Nader for President.

Robin Kolodny is assistant professor of political science at Temple University and was an APSA congressional fellow during the first session of the 104th Congress. She is the author of a forthcoming book on the congressional campaign committees and other works on American parties in comparative perspective.

Kay Lawson is professor of political science at San Francisco State University and professor associé at the Sorbonne (Paris). She is the author of *The Comparative Study of Political Parties* (1976), co-editor of *When Parties Fail* (1988), and editor of *How Political Parties Work* (1994).

Justin A. Roberts is on the board of directors of the California Reform party. He supported Ross Perot's presidential bid in 1992 and subsequently became a charter member of United We Stand America. He helped with the successful California registration drive for ballot access for the Reform party.

Terry Savage has run for office on the Libertarian party ticket, in 1994 for the California State Assembly, and in 1995 for Congress in the 13th district in California. In 1995 he was elected to state party Executive Committee, Libertarian party, and is active in charting party strategy.

Robert J. Spitzer is professor of political science at SUNY Cortland. His books include *The Right to Life Movement and Third Party Politics, President and Congress,* and *The Politics of Gun Control.*

Richard Winger has been publisher of *Ballot Access News* since 1985, and in this capacity he has researched the ballot access laws of all fifty states and the District of Columbia from 1888 to the present. He is also a field representative for the Coalition for Free and Open Elections.